Don't Blame God!

A Biblical Answer to the Problem
of Evil, Sin and Suffering

By

Mark H. Graeser

John A. Lynn

John W. Schoenheit

Note: Most Scriptures quoted in this book are from *the New International Version* (NIV). References taken from other translations or versions will be noted, i.e., *King James Version*= (KJV). In verses quoted, words in all capital letters indicate our own emphasis. Brackets [ ] in quotes from Scripture or from other authors are ours.

(NIV) = New International Version

"Scripture taken from THE HOLY BIBLE, NEW INTERNATIONAL VERSION. Copyright © 1973, 1978, 1984 International Bible Society. Used by permission of Zondervan Publishers."

International Standard Book Number: ISBN 0-9628971-2-4

FOURTH EDITION

©1994

Published by

Christian Educational Services (Referred to in footnotes as CES)

To receive our free bimonthly newsletter, *The Sower,* and/or a complete listing of our materials, please contact us at:

Christian Educational Services (CES)
2144 East 52nd Street
Indianapolis, IN 46205
888-255-6189 Fax: 317-255-6249
www.CESonline.org
CES@CESonline.org

Visit our research website at:
www.TruthOrTradition.com

Printed in the United States of America.

Table of Contents

Acknowledgments

First, and most importantly, we are thankful to our gracious and merciful Heavenly Father and our beloved Savior, Jesus Christ, for the precious gift of holy spirit and the guarantee of everlasting life. We thank God for His wonderful Word, which imparts wisdom and increases faith to all who seek its truth.

The authors accept all responsibility for the content of this book, and offer many thanks to the following people for their help in producing it.

To the people whose works we quote in this book. Although we do not agree with them on every point, we are thankful for those men and women who have diligently sought to know and share with others the truth in regard to human suffering.

To Wayne Harms for the cover design.

To Joe Ramon for his tireless service in the layout design.

To Anthony Buzzard, Robert Erasmus, Steve Keil, Judi Klug, Jim Landmark, Jon Lydell, John S. Lynn, Pat Lynn and Ivan Maddox for their assistance in editing our manuscript.

To Elaine Leonard and Pat Lynn for their diligent efforts in typing our manuscript and its many revisions.

To Suzanne Snyder for her labor of love in doing the Topical Index.

Preface

Human suffering. It is horrible. It is terrible. No one should have to go through it, yet those who escape it throughout their lives are few and far between. Ironically, the mental anguish that people go through as they ask over and over again "Why?" or "Why me?" can be as traumatic as the experience of suffering itself. Knowing the reason for suffering can go a long way toward alleviating one's anguish and helping him overcome the trauma, grief and depression often associated with it. For example, a person recovering from surgery may be in a lot of pain, but knowing the reason why he has the pain helps him get through it.

When a soldier dies on the battlefield while defending his country, it is an irreversible tragedy. We understand why he gave his life, however, and somehow that helps us deal with the situation. But when a child playing in a front yard is killed by a drunk driver, it is much harder to deal with. Unanswered "Why's" can affect the lives of people for decades. We hope to answer at least some of these "Why's," and in so doing point you toward the only real source for strength and courage in the face of adversity.

Writing this book has been extremely challenging. To begin with, the subject matter evokes the deepest emotions of the human heart. Beyond this emotional element, it involves tackling some of the most profound philosophical questions that have ever perplexed the human mind. Without a source of absolute truth from above the plane of man's opinion, these questions cannot really be answered— only pondered and discussed. In our contemplation and study of the question of why there is evil, sin and suffering, we have arrived at the conviction that the answers can be found only in the Word of God, the Bible.

Much has been written about the Bible. Many have scoffed at and doubted its truths, yet this precious Word of God has remained among us for thousands of years. Could it really be that approximately forty writers who lived in many different places during a period of 1,500 years just happened to put together a practical and historical anthology that fits together like the finest of puzzles? No, the Bible is God's holy, divinely-inspired Word (II Timothy 3:16).

II Peter 1:21 (NASV)

For no prophecy was ever made by an act of human will, but men moved by the Holy Spirit spoke from God.

The Word of God contains everything we need to know about life and godliness (II Peter 1:3). It is the words of the Creator, God, to His created beings. In it, anyone can find God's own revelation of His nature, character and purposes. Jesus Christ referred to God's Word as "truth" (John 17:17). Therefore, what follows is our attempt to set forth a wholly *biblical* answer to the problem of evil, sin and suffering.

We have tried to present this vital material in a down-to-earth way that is clear to people of all degrees of exposure to the Bible, as well as any who might be introduced to the Bible via this book. We hope you will find our work thorough yet simple, straightforward yet compassionate, sober yet joyful, and serious yet appropriately humorous.

Based upon what we know is being taught in contemporary Christianity about the reason for evil, sin and suffering, we believe that as you read this book you may be exposed to a different perspective about it than you have ever seen before. To us, it is the one that leaves the fewest questions unanswered and, most importantly, it is the perspective that we believe God has revealed in His Word. Remember that truth is not determined by whether the vast majority of people believe it, as the once-upon-a-time nearly universal "flat earth" theory so plainly proves.

Each of us must be willing to subject even our most deeply-held convictions to the scrutiny of God's written Word. In regard to the problem of evil, sin and suffering, we encourage you, as you read, to deeply consider what we believe to be a most rational alternative to what is generally referred to as "orthodox" Christian theology. Everyone applauds accuracy as essential to nearly every field of human endeavor. What endeavor could be more important to a person than accurately understanding the written revelation of his Creator? Such an understanding is the basis of one's whole attitude toward God, and affects nearly every aspect of his life.

We have not written this book to be controversial or adversarial. We have no ax to grind, nor are we striving for sensationalism by presenting the viewpoint herein. Nevertheless, we feel that the

Christian world in general has not given sound biblical answers regarding the reasons for evil, sin and suffering; that it has done more to confuse rather than enthuse its practictioners about God; and that the error promulgated has in fact aggravated the anguish that accompanies human suffering. This has caused many sincere and thoughtful people to reject the personal God of the Bible and embrace atheism, agnosticism or impersonal pagan philosophies. All such philosophical attempts to explain evil, sin and suffering are woefully inadequate, but it is not our purpose to deal with them in this book.

"How," people rightly ask, "can a God who says in the Bible that He is love be responsible for the suffering in my life and in the lives of those I love?" We hope that the scriptures we present, and our exposition of them, will clarify what God says about the whole issue of evil, sin and human suffering. By considering the entire scope of Scripture, we will endeavor to allow Him to speak for Himself and proclaim His own sterling character. Thus you can more clearly understand His heart of love for us, and in return be motivated to love and serve Him and His Son, our Lord Jesus Christ.

We are asking you, the reader, to accompany us upward on a journey to the truth, guided only by the whole of Scripture and by reason. The trail we will follow is the one suggested by these guides, though it diverges from the one most traveled. This trail is not for the complacent, nor for the lazy, because it will be a challenge. Nevertheless, the view it affords at its summit is awesome beyond words, for by taking this route one can see the very heart of God.

Some may feel threatened along the way as the trail veers from the familiar landscape of their traditional religious beliefs and heads into what, for them, is uncharted territory. Rest assured that we can follow the chart and compass of God's wonderful Word, and come with us all the way to the end, with thoughtfulness, prayer and your own study of Scripture. We believe that if you do you will see God for who He truly is, and that your heart will overflow with praise, worship and absolute reverence for Him.

In view of the magnitude of the subject, we trust you will find this is a book that can be read and studied many times. Our primary goal is to enlighten the eyes of your understanding and help you love the One True God and His Son Jesus Christ with all your heart, soul, mind and strength.

Mark H. Graeser

John A. Lynn

John W. Schoenheit

Author's note: Throughout this book there are a number of footnotes referring you to other materials available from Christian Educational Services. These teaching materials elaborate upon those points that we mention herein, but which we are not able to develop within the scope of this book. A brief description of each teaching is given at the end of the book. We heartily encourage you to take advantage of these biblical teaching materials.

INTRODUCTION

Naples Daily News
July 11, 1992

The Disabled Ponder God's Will
In a culture that glorifies physical beauty, the disabled face disquieting religious questions: Why in a world ruled by a just and loving God must they be the ones without sight, or without the use of arms and legs? [1]

The above question shows that seeking to understand human suffering is as universal as human suffering itself. It is very sad to say, but many people who do believe in God believe this one thing about Him: He must be ultimately responsible for all the suffering of mankind. Sadder still, the vast majority of *Christian* people holds the fatalistic notion that the One True God, the Father of the Lord Jesus Christ, is in control of everything that happens, good and bad. Thus they also believe, and teach, that God is responsible for all the suffering of mankind. For example:

> Though Satan is regarded as having power to make men suffer (II Cor. 12:7; Job 1:12, 2:6), they suffer only in the hand of God, and it is God who controls and sends suffering (Amos 3:6; Isa. 45:7; Matt. 26:39; Acts 2:23). [2]

Isn't the logical extension of such belief aptly expressed in this old Arab proverb: "If you see a blind man, kick him; why should you

---

1. David Briggs, *Naples Daily News* (Naples FL, July 11, 1992), page 7D.

2. *The New Bible Dictionary*, Second Edition, J. D. Douglas, Editor (Tyndale House Publishers, Inc., Wheaton IL), page 1148.

be kinder than God?"

We daresay that the question of human suffering is perhaps man's biggest obstacle to truly seeking God. Richard Rice shows why the "orthodox" Christian doctrine that God plans everything that happens only enlarges that obstacle.

> It makes God directly responsible for everything that happens— our defeats as well as our victories, our disappointments as well as our joys. In a sense, it means that only good things happen to us— some of them less pleasant than others, of course— but all of them ultimately "beneficial." From the viewpoint that God plans everything, there is no room for anything really evil.

> On the personal level, this notion is counter-intuitive. It contradicts our most fundamental convictions about the nature of things. When we experience pain or loss, we instinctively sense that something is wrong. We feel outraged, or violated, when we suffer. [3]

The Bible says in Hebrews 11:6 that if one wants to come near to God, he must believe first that He exists, and second that He is a *rewarder* of those who diligently seek Him. How many people have been discouraged from believing in God because they have been taught that the "reward" they will get from Him is evil or suffering? How much better had they been taught the truth of God's Word that when He does bless those who diligently seek Him, "He adds no trouble to it" (Proverbs 10:22). God's Word is truth, and it will give you a firm foundation to believe not only that God is love, but also that God fervently loves *you*. Once you see what He has done for you in the gift of His Son, what He wants to do for you in this life and what He will do for you in the future, you will very likely love Him in return.

In contrast to how many pagan deities are said to behave, the one true God, the Father of Jesus Christ, is not whimsical or capricious. He is not a "maybe" God. In fact, He has committed Himself to us— *in writing*! God gives every good and perfect gift, and He "does not change like shifting shadows" (James 1:17). What He promises, He will perform (Isaiah 55:10,11). Our loving heavenly

---

3. Richard Rice, *When Bad Things Happen To God's People* (Pacific Press Publishing Association, Boise ID, 1985), page 40.

Father will *always* act in perfect accord with the written revelation He has given us, and we can take His Word for it!

Numbers 23:19:

> God is not a man, that he should lie, nor a son of man, that he should change his mind. Does he speak and then not act? Does he promise and not fulfill?

God has exalted above all things His name and His Word (Psalm 138:2). God stands behind His Word. It will live and abide forever (Psalm 119:144,152). It will never fail (Matthew 5:18).

We believe that too often Christian theologians have been guilty of intellectual laziness, and thus have not arrived at rational convictions rooted in reason and faith. In the end, the truth should make sense to the logical and thoughtful person. Our fervent hope is that this book will reach some of those sincere people who have been driven from God and the Christian faith by unscriptural and misguided teaching.

Bertrand Russell, the eminent British mathematician, logician and philosopher, was a vocal critic of traditional Christian teaching. His logic is incisive, and it shows the absurdity of the concept of God's "omnipotence" as traditionally understood (we will discuss this concept later on in this book):

> There are logical difficulties in the notion of sin. We are told that sin consists in disobedience to God's commands, but we are also told that God is omnipotent. If He is, nothing contrary to His will can occur; therefore, when the sinner disobeys His commands, He must have intended this to happen. St. Augustine boldly accepts this view, and asserts that men are led to sin by a blindness with which God afflicts them. But most theologians in modern times have felt that if God causes men to sin, it is not fair to send them to "hell" for what they cannot help.

> We are told that sin consists in acting contrary to God's will. This, however, does not get rid of the difficulty. Those who, like Spinoza, take God's omnipotence seriously, deduce that there can be no such thing as sin. This leads to frightful results. "What?!" said Spinoza's contemporaries, "Was it not wicked of Nero to murder his mother?"...If everything happens in accordance with God's will, God must have wanted

Nero to murder his mother; therefore, since God is good, the murder must have been a good thing. From this argument there is no escape. [4]

Actually, Lord Russell concedes that saying that God is not omnipotent "gets [us] out of all the logical puzzles." However, as an agnostic, with no belief in the Word of God he then asks:

How are we to know what is really God's will? If the forces of evil have a certain share of power, they may deceive us into accepting as Scripture what is really their work. This was the view of the Gnostics, who thought that the Old Testament was the work of an evil spirit.

As soon as we abandon our own reason, and are content to rely upon authority, there is no end to our troubles. Whose authority? The Old Testament? The New Testament? The Koran? [5]

To Lord Russell, and others whose reason and intellect has brought them at odds with such inconsistent and contradictory teaching of traditional Christianity, we offer the following thought: If the whole Bible is the Word of God, it cannot contradict itself, or it is shown to be a fraud, for it purports to be authored by the One who is also the Author of reason and logic.

Rather than abandon our reason in favor of a blind, irrational "faith," we will cling tenaciously to the premise that the God of the Bible cannot contradict Himself nor act contrary to His own nature. In one way of looking at it, God submits Himself to His word. Therefore we will pursue, with as much honesty and vigor as we can muster, the intellectual integrity of the Scriptures as they were originally communicated by "holy men of God" (II Peter 1:21). If this conviction in the rationality of God and His Word leads us into non-traditional or unorthodox ways of thinking, so be it.

Our main objective in writing this book is, as stated earlier, to enlighten the eyes of your understanding regarding evil, sin and suffering and help you love the One True God and His Son with all your heart, soul, mind and strength. In order to do this, we will set forth from Scripture what God has revealed to us about His nature.

---

4. Bertrand Russell, *Unpopular Essays*, "An Outline of Intellectual Rubbish" (Simon & Schuster, New York NY, 1950), page 80.

5. *Ibid.*, page 81.

You will see that God is love and that God is righteous, and that therefore His character is unblemished. You will see that God is not the cause [6] of evil,[7] of sin [8] or of suffering. [9]

We will show that the reason for human suffering is *sin*— the Devil's, Adam's and man's, that suffering is a result of these sins, and that therefore suffering is a fact of life. You will see that each human is born into an extensive and ongoing spiritual battle, and that those who believe on the Lord Jesus Christ have not only been guaranteed the final victory, but also have been equipped to be victorious in this life.

You will see from Scripture that in the midst of "this present evil age," each Christian is tested daily. The Bible teaches that Satan tests us by trying to steal, kill and destroy, and that God tests us by asking us to trust and obey Him, for our own ultimate benefit, as

---

6. "cause"— The word "cause" contains complexities that need to be understood by any student of the Bible. In its simplest sense, the "cause" of something is that which makes the difference between whether or not that something occurs. Beyond that, an important distinction must be made between *necessary conditions* and *sufficient causes*. For instance, for a fire to occur, oxygen and fuel must be present. These are necessary conditions, without which fire cannot occur, but they are not sufficient causes for a fire start. The sufficient cause of fire is enough *heat* to kindle the fuel.

Another concept to be understood is the difference between an immediate cause and a remote cause. In the case of a fire in a warehouse, the immediate cause may have been ignited gasoline, but the remote cause was that the owner set the fire himself to collect insurance money to pay his gambling debts. In such a case, we make the distinction between a "reason" and a "cause." The *cause* of the fire was the owner's actions, but the *reason* or motive was his gambling debt.

While God's actions are sometimes the immediate cause of some suffering or even death (as in cases like the Flood, the destruction of Sodom and Gomorrah, etc.), He is never the remote cause or the reason for it. He always acts in the best interests of mankind, generally and specifically, and is only the cause of suffering and death when these are a necessary by-product of His righteous, redemptive activity. He takes no pleasure in afflicting, harming, or punishing people, even His enemies, and is *never* the reason for these things occurring (Ezekiel 18:23, 32; 33:11). *Sin* is the necessary condition for any kind of suffering to occur, whatever the immediate cause may be— God, the Devil, or oneself.

Finally, the concept of an occasional cause needs to be understood, for it gives insight into why God is sometimes viewed as the "cause" of suffering. An "occasional cause" is a person or circumstance that precedes an effect, and who or which, without being the real cause, is the occasion of its action. God's Word often is the "immovable object," or the occasion that "causes" people's suffering (E.g., see Romans 7:1-12). For further study of the word "cause," see: Irving M. Copi, *Introduction To Logic* (MacMillan Pub. Co., New York NY, 1978, 5th edition), pages 400-404.

would any loving Father. We will see that sometimes obedience to God requires sacrifice, or suffering at the hands of evil. But this can result in great individual growth in faith, hope and love, because God and His Son Jesus Christ are always beside us in the trenches of life, responding to our trials and tribulations with comfort, direction and supernatural assistance. As Richard Rice states:

> We are important to God. He cares for us so much that everything about us matters to Him... someone who is truly concerned about your welfare cannot avoid taking an active interest in your life. As the Bible indicates, God's involvement in human affairs continued long after Creation week ended, and it expresses the same motive that led Him to create human beings and the world in which they live. [10]

Also, you will see that obedience in the face of trials can help us better identify with Jesus Christ, and that our faithfulness lays up rewards that will be given to us at Christ's appearing. It can also result in great benefit in the lives of others who see our godly examples.

If we succeed in achieving the above objectives, you the reader should benefit in several ways. You should grow in *love*, in *faith* and in *hope*. The truths of God's Word set forth in this book should help you grow in *love* for the wonderful God who so loved you that He gave His only begotten Son for you, and for Jesus Christ who gave His life for you. These truths should also enable you to stand in the stead of Christ to empathize with and love other people, both Christians and "not yet" Christians.

In Hosea 4:6, regarding why calamity had come upon Israel, God said, "My people are destroyed from lack of knowledge."

An accurate knowledge of God's Word is your only basis for genuine *faith* in God. You can *know* that God and His Son are always fighting for you. Then, no matter what life's circumstances, you can turn to them with growing faith, faith undiluted by the fatalistic

---

7. "evil"— active opposition to that which is good, that is, godly.

8. "sin"— (a) an act of disobedience to God (b) man's state of spiritual separation from God caused by Adam's original act of disobedience.

9. "suffering"— In the context of this book, we define "suffering" as mental or physical pain or anguish.

10. Rice, *When Bad Things Happen To God's People*, page 22.

misconception that everything, good and bad, comes from God. You can be confident that He and His Son want to help you even more than you want them to. Knowing these truths in God's Word will generate in you great hope for deliverance in this life, and greatly magnify your *hope* of living forever in Paradise [11] with Jesus Christ and all who will have ever believed in Him.

We doubt that most people really *want* to worship and serve a God who is responsible for evil and human suffering. But what about a God Who is all love and Who is at work in every situation to help everyone He can? "Ya gotta love a God like that!" And you can.

---

11. *The Kingdom of God: Paradise Regained* (CES Bi-Monthly Tape, Mar/Apr 1992).

CHAPTER 1

IS GOD THE PROBLEM?

Traditional Explanations Fall Short

Have you ever asked, or heard anyone else ask: "If God is so 'loving,' why is there so much suffering in the world?" Or, "Why is life so unfair?" Or, "What have I done to deserve this?" Or, "How can God allow babies to be born deformed?" Or, "Why doesn't God do something about all the misery of humanity?" (Of course, some people say He *is* doing something— He's *adding* to it!).

Traditional Christianity has failed to provide satisfactory answers to these questions. [12] Today, a great deal of what is represented as Christianity is, in reality, "religion," that is, the doctrines and commandments of men.

---

12. We would like to say a word to our Christian brothers and sisters who have handled distressing and difficult times by taking comfort in the belief that everything that happens to us is somehow the will of God. If this is you, our book may *at first* leave you feeling open and exposed. If so, please persevere and withhold your judgment until you have read the whole book. You will see that not everything that happens to us is the will of God, but the Christian who stands firm in the faith will eventually see that we have a God who turns "lemons into lemonade."

"Religion" does purport to answer the above questions. For example: "The bad things happening to you must be because you're a bad person or because you have sinned, and God is punishing you." Or, "This sickness is God testing your faith." Or, "God allowed that tragedy to humble you and strengthen your faith." Or, "This terrible situation is how God is breaking your pride." In reality, such "answers" only add to man's already unbearable burdens.

Millions of people accept such erroneous ideas, and it is not because atheists tell them so, unless perhaps they are atheistic lawyers or insurance agents who, acquiescing to the jargon of their trades, often describe many natural catastrophes as "acts of God." Sometimes it seems that just about the only folks who *don't* hold God accountable for human suffering are atheists. Well, at least they have one thing right.

How sad that so many *Christian* people also attribute to God these traumatic occurrences, as well as accidents, persecution, disease and death. One reason they do is because other sincere but misinformed Christians have failed to understand God's wonderful Word, and have thus distorted it. These erroneous teachings have not only wounded people emotionally, but also turned them away from the *only* true source of comfort, strength, wisdom *and* supernatural deliverance, which is God, through His Son Jesus Christ. The fact is, the teaching that God causes suffering causes more suffering. As we will see, an accurate biblical understanding of the origin of evil and suffering relieves God of all responsibility for it.

The Problem With Blaming God

At this point we feel it is appropriate to quote at some length from the book *When Bad Things Happen To Good People,* by Rabbi Harold Kushner. This is a book well worth reading. In the first chapter, "Why Do The Righteous Suffer?" the author sets forth a number of familiar answers to this question, and why they leave much to be desired. Although we feel that Kushner's book itself does not adequately answer this question, his insight, especially in the first chapter, is most pertinent to our subject.

Kushner addresses seven commonly held "reasons" as to why people suffer, which are as follows:

1. We deserve what we get.

2. People do in fact get what they deserve, but only over the course of time.

3. God has His reasons for making people suffer, reasons that they are in no position to judge.

4. Suffering is educational.

5. Suffering is just a test.

6. Suffering comes to liberate us from pain and lead us to a better place [after death].

7. An all-powerful God does not necessarily have to be fair and just, from our limited human perspective. [13]

Kushner elaborates upon these reasons:

One of the ways in which people have tried to make sense of the world's suffering in every generation has been by assuming that we deserve what we get, that somehow our misfortunes come as punishment for our sins...

It is tempting at one level to believe that bad things happen to people (especially other people) because God is a righteous judge who gives them exactly what they deserve. By believing that, we keep the world orderly and understandable. We give people the best possible reason for being good and for avoiding sin. And by believing that, we can maintain an image of God as all-loving, all-powerful and totally in control...

The idea that God gives people what they deserve, that our misdeeds cause our misfortune, is a neat and attractive solution to the problem of evil at several levels, but it has a number of serious limitations. As we have seen, it teaches people to blame themselves. It creates guilt even where there is no basis for guilt. It makes people hate God, even as it makes them hate themselves. And most disturbing of all, it does not even fit the facts...

Sometimes we try to make sense of life's trials by saying that people do in fact get what they deserve, but only over the

---

13. Rabbi Harold Kushner, *When Bad Things Happen To Good People* (Avon Books, New York NY, 1981), pages 9, 12, 14, 19, 24, 26, 27, 40.

course of time. At any given moment, life may seem unfair
and innocent people may appear to be suffering. But if we
wait long enough, we believe, we will see the righteousness
of God's plan emerge. [14]

Often, victims of misfortune try to console themselves with
the idea that God has His reasons for making this happen to
them, reasons that they are in no position to judge. [15]

There is much that is moving in this suggestion, and I can
imagine that many people would find it comforting. Point-
less suffering, suffering as punishment for some unspecified
sin, is hard to bear. But suffering as a contribution to a great
work of art designed by God Himself may be seen, not only
as a tolerable burden, but even as a privilege. [16]

On closer examination, however, this approach is found
wanting. For all its compassion, it too is based in large
measure on wishful thinking. The crippling illness of a child,
the death of a young husband and father, the ruin of an
innocent person through malicious gossip— these are all
real. We have seen them. [17]

How seriously would we take a person who said, "I have
faith in Adolf Hitler, or in John Dillinger. I can't explain why
they did the things they did, but I can't believe they would
have done them without a good reason." Yet people try to
justify the deaths and tragedies God [supposedly] inflicts on
innocent victims with almost these same words.

Furthermore, my religious commitment to the supreme value
of an individual life makes it hard for me to accept an answer
that is not scandalized by an innocent person's pain, that

14. *Ibid.*, pages 9-12. Kushner rightly points out that the argument that "we get what
we deserve in this life if we wait long enough" is patently false, because countless
people go to their graves without having seen their unfair suffering cease. What he
fails to point out is that "long enough" primarily regards life in the age to come,
when the justice of God will prevail and, thankfully, the suffering of God's people
will end. At that time, the saved will see God's justice dealt to the wicked (Matthew
5:11,12; Romans 2:5-11; II Thessalonians 1:6,7; II Peter 2:1-10).

15. *Ibid.*, page 14.

16. *Ibid.*, page 18.

17. *Ibid.*, page 18.

condones human pain because it supposedly contributes to an overall work of esthetic value. If a human artist or employer made children suffer so that something immensely impressive or valuable could come to pass, we would put him in prison. Why then should we excuse God for causing such undeserved pain, no matter how wonderful the ultimate result may be? [18]

This is a very valid point that should to be taken to heart. It seems that the idea that "God has His reasons," even though we do not understand them, is the single most common excuse that people give as to why God causes suffering. For example, writing about the biblical character Job, Philip Yancey stated: "In some mysterious way, Job's terrible ordeal was 'worth' it to God..." [19] "Mysterious" indeed, so mysterious that even God Himself apparently does not understand this concept well enough to explain it anywhere in Scripture.

It is a common moral axiom in our society that "the end does not justify the means." Getting an "A" on a test does not justify cheating. Winning a race does not justify using steroids. Getting a job does not justify killing the other job applicants. In the Bible, God spends a lot of time defining what is moral and holy behavior. He makes it clear that a good end does not justify evil means (Romans 3:8). One place where God makes this point, using an analogy, is in II Timothy: "...if anyone competes as an athlete, he does not receive the victor's crown unless he competes according to the rules" (II Timothy 2:5).

Does the God who teaches us that the end does not justify the means then deal with us as if it did? We think not. If God is somehow responsible for mankind's misery, if He could stop it but doesn't, if He has "reasons" because somehow this is all part of some unseen "plan" that will work to His glory, then He does not practice what He preaches.

---

18. *Ibid.*, page 19. The fact is that very few people really do excuse God. Most feel angry, hurt and betrayed. Their tragedy (bad enough by itself) and their anger toward God are then compounded by the guilt they feel for being angry at God. Furthermore, they have no basis to ask God to relieve their suffering. This is how terribly frustrating life can become due to error about God's Word in regard to evil, sin and suffering.

19. Philip Yancey, *Disappointment With God* (Harper Paperbacks, New York NY, 1991), page 249.

In this vein, Rabbi Kushner comments on the "educational" value of suffering:

> Let us now consider another question: Can suffering be educational? Can it cure us of our faults and make us better people? Sometimes religious people...would like to believe that God has good reasons for making us suffer... [20]

> The problem with a line of reasoning like this one is that it isn't really meant to help the sufferer or to explain his suffering. It is meant primarily to defend God, to use words and ideas to transform bad into good and pain into privilege. Such answers are thought up by people who believe very strongly that God is a loving parent who controls what happens to us, and on the basis of that belief adjust and interpret the facts to fit their assumption. It may be true that surgeons stick knives into people to help them, but not everyone who sticks a knife into somebody else is a surgeon. It may be true that sometimes we have to do painful things to people we love for their benefit, but not every painful thing that happens to us is beneficial.

> I would find it easier to believe that I experience tragedy and suffering in order to "repair" that which is faulty in my personality if there were some clear connection between the fault and the punishment. A parent who disciplines a child for doing something wrong, but never tells him what he is being punished for, is hardly a model of responsible parent-hood. Yet, those who explain suffering as God's way of teaching us to change are at a loss to specify just what it is about us we are supposed to change. [21]

> We have all read stories of little children who were left unwatched for just a moment and fell from a window or into a swimming pool and died. Why does God permit such a thing to happen to an innocent child? It can't be to teach a child a lesson about exploring new areas. By the time the lesson is over, the child is dead. Is it to teach the parents and baby-sitters to be more careful? That is too trivial a lesson to be purchased at the price of a child's life. Is it to make the

20. Kushner, *When Bad Things Happen To Good People*, page 19.

21. *Ibid.*, page 23.

parents more sensitive, more compassionate people, more appreciative of life and health because of their experience? Is it to move them to work for better safety standards, and in that way save a hundred future lives? The price is still too high, and the reasoning shows too little regard for the value of an individual life. I am offended by those who suggest that God creates retarded children so that those around them will learn compassion and gratitude. Why should God distort someone else's life to such a degree in order to enhance my spiritual sensitivity? [22]

We too are offended by such preposterous ideas. The value of one human life is a lesson well taught in Scripture, especially in many of the parables of Jesus. What was the lesson of the one lost sheep? What was the value of the one lost coin? Was it not the importance of one individual to God? The following verses corroborate this truth:

Deuteronomy 32:9-11

For the Lord's portion is his people, Jacob his allotted inheritance.

In a desert land he found him, in a barren and howling waste. He shielded him and cared for him; he guarded him as the apple of his eye,

Like an eagle that stirs up its nest and hovers over its young, that spreads its wings to catch them and carries them on its pinions.

Addressing the commonly held belief that suffering is God testing us, Kushner writes:

If we cannot satisfactorily explain suffering by saying we deserve what we get, or by viewing it as a "cure" for our faults, can we accept the interpretation of tragedy as a test?...[Many believe that] God sends such tests and afflictions only to people He knows are capable of handling them, so that they and others can learn the extent of their spiritual strength.

Does God "temper the wind to the shorn lamb"? Does He never ask more of us than we can endure? My experience,

22. *Ibid.*, page 24.

alas, has been otherwise. I have seen people crack under the strain of unbearable tragedy. I have seen marriages break up after the death of a child, because parents blamed each other for not taking proper care or for carrying the defective gene, or simply because the memories they shared were unendurably painful. I have seen some people made noble and sensitive through suffering, but I have seen many more people grow cynical and bitter. I have seen people become jealous of those around them, unable to take part in the routines of normal living. I have seen cancers and automobile accidents take the life of one member of a family, and functionally end the lives of five others, who could never again be the normal, cheerful people they were before disaster struck. If God is testing us, He must know by now that many of us fail the test. If He is only giving us burdens we can bear, I have seen Him miscalculate far too often. [23]

Kushner expresses excellent insight about the rationalizations necessitated by such false premises:

Sometimes in our reluctance to admit that there is unfairness in the world, we try to persuade ourselves that what has happened is not really bad. We only think that it is. It is only our selfishness that makes us cry because five-year-old Michael is [supposedly] with God instead of living with us. Sometimes, in our cleverness, we try to persuade ourselves that what we call evil is not real, does not really exist, but is only a condition of not enough goodness, even as "cold" means "not enough heat," or darkness is a name we give to the absence of light. We may thus "prove" that there is really no such thing as darkness or cold, but people do stumble and hurt themselves because of the dark, and people do die of exposure to cold. Their deaths and injuries are no less real because of our verbal cleverness. [24]

In summation, Kushner states:

All the responses to tragedy which we have considered have at least one thing in common. They all assume that God is the cause of our suffering, and they try to understand why God

23. *Ibid.*, pages 24-26.

24. *Ibid.*, pages 27,28.

would want us to suffer. Is it for our own good, or is it a punishment we deserve, or could it be that God does not care what happens to us? Many of the answers were sensitive and imaginative, but none was totally satisfying. Some led us to blame ourselves in order to spare God's reputation. Others asked us to deny reality or to repress our true feelings. We were left either hating ourselves for deserving such a fate, or hating God for sending it to us when we did not deserve it. [25]

Kushner is so right in saying that semantic shenanigans have not given us satisfying answers to the problem of human suffering. Unfortunately, much of this cleverness has been presented as being the truth of God's Word. As E.G. White accurately observes, these manmade theories presented as biblical doctrine drive people away from God.

The errors of popular theology have driven many a soul to skepticism who might otherwise have been a believer in Scripture. It is impossible for him to accept doctrines which outrage his sense of justice, mercy, and benevolence; and since these are represented as the teachings of the Bible, he refuses to receive it as the Word of God. [26]

Darwin's Dilemma

One man who turned away from God because he could not reconcile a loving God with the suffering he saw all around him was Charles Darwin, whose unbelief eventually contributed significantly to the development of his so-called "theory of evolution," a myth that has blinded many to the truth of God's Word. [27] In the January 1992 issue of *Impact* (published by the Institute For Creation Research), John Morris wrote about Darwin's dilemma as to how certain complex parts of the human body could have come about by chance:

---

25. *Ibid.*, page 29.

26. E.G. White, *Final War* (Inspiration Books, Phoenix AZ, Reprinted 1979), page 70.

27. For an overview of the creation-evolution controversy, an explanation of why the theory of evolution is scientifically preposterous, and an explanation of what the Bible says about creation, we refer you to the audio cassette seminar, *The Creation-Evolution Controversy* (available from CES).

A favorite example of obvious design has always been the human eye. With its many functioning parts—the lens, cornea, iris, etc., the controlling muscles, the sensitive rods and cones which translate light energy into chemical signals, the optic nerve which speeds these signals to a decoding center in the brain—and on and on. The eye was unquestionably designed by an incredibly intelligent Designer who had a complete grasp of optical physics.

Darwin was frustrated by the eye's complexity, even though he knew only a fraction of what scientists have now discovered about the eye. In his book, *Origin of Species,* he included a section entitled, "Organs of Extreme Perfection and Complication," in which he declared: "To suppose that the eye, with all its inimitable contrivances for adjusting the focus to different amounts of light, and for the correction of spherical and chromatic aberration, could have been formed by natural selection, seems, I freely confess, absurd in the highest degree." Yet in the next several pages, he discussed how he thought it might have happened.

One may wonder why Darwin was forced to adopt and defend what he admitted was an absurd conclusion. His reasoning is made plain in the following quote. Keep in mind that Darwin was raised in a nominally religious home, but whose extended family had a well established anti-Christian perspective. Darwin, himself, studied for the ministry, as was common in those days for individuals of a scholarly bent, but eventually rejected the Christian faith.

In a May 22, 1860 letter to Professor Asa Gray of Harvard, propagator of evolution on the American continent, Darwin wrote, evidently to answer Gray's advocacy of "theistic" evolution: "I had no intention to write atheistically. But I own that I cannot see as plainly as others do, and as I should wish to do, evidence of design and beneficence [goodness] on all sides of us. There seems to me to be TOO MUCH MISERY IN THE WORLD [Emphasis ours]. I cannot persuade myself that a beneficent and omnipotent God would have designedly created the ichneumonidae [parasites] with the express intention of their feeding within the living bodies of caterpillars, or that a cat should play with mice. Not believing this, I see no necessity in the belief that the eye was expressly designed." [28]

It is noteworthy that Darwin studied for the ministry, but eventually rejected the Christian faith. Apparently, whatever he was taught laid the blame for human suffering on God. Not being able to bring himself to believe that "a beneficent and omnipotent God" could be responsible for the suffering in the world, he concluded that there must be *no* God. If the teaching Darwin received was anything like what most Christians have been taught about this subject, his disillusionment is understandable. Only God knows how many millions of others have turned away from Him for this same reason.

At one time in his life, nearly everyone asks questions about evil, sin and suffering such as those we mentioned at the beginning of this chapter. Asking the right questions is a big key to getting the right answers. We agree with Kushner's suggestion that too many people may very well have been asking the wrong questions:

> Could it be that God does not cause the bad things that happen to us? Could it be that He doesn't decide which families shall give birth to a handicapped child, that He did not single out Ron to be crippled by a bullet or Helen by a degenerative disease, but rather that He stands ready to help them and us cope with our tragedies if we could only get beyond the feelings of guilt and anger that separate us from Him? Could it be that "How could God do this to me?" is really the wrong question for us to ask? [29]

We will now attempt to ask the right questions and do our best to show you the biblical answers to them.

---

28. John Morris, "Natural Selection Versus Supernatural Design," *Impact* (Institute For Creation Research, El Cajon CA 92021, January 1992).

29. Kushner, *When Bad Things Happen To Good People*, page 30.

CHAPTER 2

SIN IS THE PROBLEM

Who Sinned?

Ever wondered why it's called an "alarm" clock? Maybe it's because it signals the start of another day filled with the possibility of facing many "alarming" situations. But why? Why must we all awaken day after day to countless possibilities of trauma? The answer is *sin*, which is disobedience to God. But *whose* sin? We will answer that question later, but can you think of anywhere in the Bible that people asked it? How about the ninth chapter of John, where Jesus and His disciples encountered a man born blind?

John 9:1,2 (KJV)

And as Jesus passed by, he saw a man which was blind from *his* birth.

And his disciples asked him, saying, Master, who did sin, this man or his parents, that he was born blind?

At the time of Christ, some rabbis taught that a person could sin in a previous life, or even in the womb. [30] That accounts for the disciples' question, "Who did sin, this man . . . that he was born blind?" Millions of other people have also asked "Who sinned" in regard to similarly grievous situations.

For new parents to hear their doctor say, "Your son is blind," would be anguish no words can describe. Many parents who have had to face such tragedy have had it compounded by someone's presumptuous proclamation that it was their own sin that brought it upon them. Was that what Jesus said? Not at all.

John 9:3,4 (KJV)

Jesus answered, Neither hath this man sinned, nor his parents: but that the works of God should be made manifest in him.

I must work the works of him that sent me, while it is day: the night cometh, when no man can work.

Although Jesus did not answer the question "Who sinned?" He did make it clear that it was neither the man nor his parents. Furthermore, Jesus did *not* say that it was the work of God that the man was blind. In fact, Jesus emphasized that the will of God was to *rectify* the situation, which He then proceeded to do by healing the man.

Every student of Scripture should be aware that the theology and beliefs of the translators of any version of the Bible affected the way they translated it. Most Greek and Hebrew words have a range of meanings (just as most English words do) and can be translated several different ways. Furthermore, there was no punctuation in the early biblical manuscripts. All the words were run together without breaks between them, and without periods, commas, etc. All punctuation was added by translators through the years, as were chapter and verse numbers.

Unfortunately, most translators through the centuries have believed that God is the cause of evil, sin and suffering. The punctuation that has been added to John 9:3,4 in the modern Greek texts, from which we get most of our English translations, reflects

---

30. John Lightfoot, *A Commentary On The New Testament From The Talmud and Hebraica* (Vol. 3, Luke-John), (Oxford Press, 1859, reprinted 1989 by Hendrickson Publishers, Inc.), page 340.

this. They do indeed make it seem as if God had made the man blind at birth so He could later heal him, but that would be like a car dealer selling a new car with broken headlights so as to later be able to show off the quality of its service department. The NIV translation is perhaps easier to understand, but is it accurate?

John 9:3,4

"Neither this man nor his parents sinned," said Jesus, "but this happened so that the work of God might be displayed in his life.

As long as it is day, we must do the work of him who sent me. Night is coming, when no one can work."

Look back at the King James Version's rendering of John 9:3,4. In verse 3, we would put a period after the word "parents" and a comma after the word "him." Thus the text would read, "Neither hath this man sinned, nor his parents. But that the works of God should be made manifest in him, I must work the works of him that sent me...."

We feel that in his translation of the New Testament titled *The Message*, Eugene Peterson captures the heart of these verses:

John 9:3,4

Jesus said, "You're asking the wrong question. You're looking for someone to blame. There is no such cause-effect here. Look instead for what God can do. We need to be energetically at work for the One Who sent me here, working while the sun shines. When night falls, the workday is over."

Religious tradition teaches that God is glorified when a believer nobly endures sickness or suffering. Jesus apparently believed that God is more glorified by delivering people from such trauma.

If people are going to be delivered, someone must work the works of God. Neither the parents nor the man had sinned. Nor had God made the man blind just so He could heal him later (after years of suffering). Jesus did not answer the disciples' question as to the cause of the problem. He did, however, show them, and the blind man, God's solution. Since Jesus did not answer the question of who sinned that the man was born blind, can we find the answer elsewhere in Scripture? Yes, so let us start "in the beginning."

"I Love Lucifer"

Scripture teaches that God *is* love and, since His character is constant, He has *always been* love. God is light and in Him is no darkness at all. His purposes and His plans are righteous. He is "holy," meaning that He is separate from His creation. God is not tainted by a sin-stained creation, provided it can be shown from His Word that He is in no way responsible for its having been stained.

What was the decision that God faced "in the beginning" as He contemplated His future creation? It was whether or not to create independent free-will beings with not only the capacity to reciprocate His love, but also the capacity to reject it and turn against Him. One is not possible without the other. As E.G. White put it:

> The law of love being the foundation of the government of God, the happiness of all created beings depended upon their perfect accord with its great principles of righteousness. God desires from all His creatures the service of love— homage that springs from an intelligent appreciation of His character. He takes no pleasure in a forced allegiance, and to all He grants freedom of will, that they may render Him voluntary service. [31]

It seems logical that before God made the decision to create living beings with freedom of will, He had to plan for their possible failure. We believe that in His infinitely diversified wisdom He contemplated every conceivable eventuality and formulated a contingency plan for each, with a view toward His desired goal for mankind. He decided to "go for it," and because God's nature is pure righteousness, in His acts of creating such beings He knowingly and willingly committed Himself to a totally *righteous* dealing with all of them, even if they chose to rebel against Him.

As far as we know from Scripture, the first beings created by God were angels (Job 38:4-7). One of the most powerful is referred to in the Bible as "Lucifer." [32] Although he was an awesome and powerful being, Lucifer was not made morally perfect. That is, he

---

31. White, *Final War*, page 2.

32. The Hebrew word translated "Lucifer" in Isaiah 14:12 (KJV) actually means "shining star." The Latin Vulgate translated the Hebrew as "Lucifer," which made its way into the Roman Catholic Douay Version and into the King James Version.

had free will, he could either obey God or disobey Him, and it was up to him to choose between these two alternatives. Speaking figuratively about Lucifer's beauty, wisdom and ability, Ezekiel wrote:

Ezekiel 28:12-15

Son of man, take up a lament concerning the king of Tyre [Satan [33]] and say to him: This is what the Sovereign Lord says: "You were the model of perfection, full of wisdom and perfect in beauty.

You were in Eden, the garden of God; every precious stone adorned you: ruby, topaz and emerald, chrysolite, onyx and jasper, sapphire, turquoise and beryl. Your settings and mountings were made of gold; on the day you were created they were prepared.

You were anointed as a guardian cherub, for so I ordained you. You were on the holy mount of God; you walked among the fiery stones.

You were blameless in your ways from the day you were created till wickedness was found in you."

Some will ask,"How could Lucifer have even conceived of evil?" This is a very good question, and we believe the answer lies in the above verses. First of all, remember that God created him with genuine freedom of will. Second, God in His goodness had made Lucifer so magnificent that you could say he had a taste of what it was like to be God.

The question could be asked: Why didn't God create Lucifer with less ability and wisdom, in order to protect Himself against the consequences of his potential rebellion? The only answer we can

---

33. The phrase "King of Tyre" is put for Satan by the figure of speech Antonomasia. Antonomasia is a common figure of speech. *The World Book Dictionary* defines it as follows: "1. The use of an epithet, title, etc., instead of a person's name, as to refer to an ambassador as 'his Excellency,' or to a judge as 'his Honor.' 2. The use of a proper name to express a quality, as to call a patient person 'a veritable Job.' " E.W. Bullinger expands this and gives more examples: "As when a name of some office, dignity, profession, science, or trade is used instead of the proper name of the person, *e.g.*, when we speak of the Queen as *Her Majesty*, or of a nobleman as *his lordship*; or when a wise man is called *a solon*, or *a Solomon*, etc. When we speak of David as 'the Psalmist,' or of Paul as 'the Apostle,' we use the figure *Antonomasia*." E.W. Bullinger, *Figures Of Speech Used In The Bible*. (page 682). In this case, the "King of Tyre" is not the human king, but rather the one who is the "prince of this age" (II Cor. 4:4), the Devil.

think of lies in the phrase "the model of perfection" in Ezekiel 28. The KJV reads, "thou sealest up the sum," which E.W. Bullinger translates "thou art the finished pattern." Lucifer was the finished pattern, or the model of perfection, for a created being. That is, God gave him all the capacity for wisdom and understanding that He could give a created being.

Among all God's creation, Lucifer was most capable of perceiving God's nature and goodness, having been made most like Him. But instead of appreciating the grace of this exalted station and enjoying the fellowship available with God, he was lifted up in pride, thinking himself to be deserving of even greater status— that due only the Creator Himself. He was close enough to being like God that he thought equality with God was something he could grab. [34]

Making Lucifer "the model of perfection, full of wisdom and perfect in beauty" was an expression of God's magnanimity, and to His credit. Lucifer should have been filled with thanksgiving and praise for his Creator, and eager to serve Him in response to God's blessings. Instead, pride in his own greatness fueled his desire for supremacy. All he ever said was, "I love Lucifer." His pride finally drove him to attempt to usurp God's ultimate authority. Isaiah speaks of Lucifer's ambitions:

Isaiah 14:13,14

You said in your heart, I WILL ascend to heaven; I WILL raise my throne above the stars of God; I WILL sit enthroned on the mount of assembly, on the utmost heights of the sacred mountain.

I WILL ascend above the tops of the clouds; I WILL make myself like the Most High. [35]

---

34. Philippians 2:6-11 makes it clear that Jesus, though He was adorned with holy spirit without measure and shared in God's divine nature, never pridefully aspired to a higher position than that of a servant to others. Rather, He sought to serve His Father and Creator, not thinking that "equality with God was something to be grasped," as had Lucifer. God responded to His Son's heart-felt humility and obedience by not just exalting Him, but by highly exalting Him to functional equality with Himself, making him worthy of honor, worship and praise.

35. Some have doubted whether Isaiah 14:12-17 actually refers to a spirit being that warred with God and now is known as the Devil. We find the textual and contextual evidence compelling, and refer the reader to some of the good work on the subject that has already been done by men such as E.W. Bullinger, C.C. Ryrie and C. I.

It is obvious that Lucifer had freedom of will, because five times he said, "I will." But God will have the last word. [36] The impending doom of the Devil is certain, and many verses attest to that fact. God responded to Lucifer's pride and rebellion by driving him from His presence and casting him to earth.

Ezekiel 28:16,17

Through your widespread trade you were filled with violence, and you sinned. So I drove you in disgrace from the mount of God, and I expelled you, O guardian cherub, from among the fiery stones.

Your heart became proud on account of your beauty, and you corrupted your wisdom because of your splendor. So I threw you to the earth; I made a spectacle of you before kings. [37]

As a result of his fall, Lucifer became the chief antagonist of mankind. He is called by many names in Scripture. He is called "the Devil" (Revelation 20:2— *diabolos* literally means "slanderer"), "Satan" (Luke 22:31— the Greek word *satanas* comes from the Hebrew *satan*, which means "adversary"), "Belial" (II Corinthians 6:15— it means "worthless," and is used in connection with filthiness and wickedness), "serpent" (Genesis 3:1— to emphasize his evil craftiness), "dragon" (Revelation 20:2— to emphasize his evil and power), "tempter" (Matthew 4:3), "accuser" (Revelation 12:10), "evil one" (Matthew 6:13), "god of this age" (II Corinthians 4:4), "prince (John 12:31— ruler; Greek=*arche*) of this world," "prince of demons" (Mark 3:22), and "the ruler of the kingdom of the air" (Ephesians 2:2). As the amount of evil and suffering on earth attests, the Devil is doing an excellent job of living up to his biblical names.

Why didn't God destroy Satan at the time of his original rebellion? Another good question. We believe E.G. White offers a plausible explanation:

Scofield. Godly men have long recognized the need for reading the Scriptures with a spiritual sensitivity, because a number of verses in the Bible have both a present and future application. Two such examples are Hosea 11:1 and Psalm 69:9. Modern critics ignorantly laugh at Matthew's "fanciful exegesis" of Hosea 11:1 (see Matthew 2:15) or John's "ignoring context" in interpreting Psalm 69:9 (see John 2:17), but we accept the text as authoritative.

36. In the KJV of Ezekiel 28:16-18, God says "I will" six times in relation to how He will one day, once and for all, dispose of the Devil.

37. The last clause is still future, and shows us that Satan's original defeat foreshadows his eventual destruction.

Even when it was decided that he could no longer remain in Heaven, infinite wisdom did not destroy Satan. Since the service of love can alone be acceptable to God, the allegiance of His creatures must rest upon a conviction of His justice and benevolence. The inhabitants of Heaven,... being unprepared to comprehend the nature or consequences of sin, could not then have seen the justice and mercy of God in the destruction of Satan. Had he been immediately blotted from existence, they would have served God from fear, rather than from love. The influence of the deceiver would not have been fully destroyed, nor would the spirit of rebellion have been utterly eradicated. Evil must be permitted to come to maturity. For the good of the entire universe through ceaseless ages, Satan must more fully develop his principles, that his charges against the divine government might be seen in their true light by all created beings, that the justice and mercy of God and the immutability of His law might forever be placed beyond all question.

Satan's rebellion was to be a lesson to the universe through all coming ages, a perpetual testimony to the nature and terrible results of sin. The working out of Satan's rule, its effects upon both men and angels, would show what must be the fruit of setting aside the divine authority. It would testify that with the existence of God's government and His Law is bound up the well-being of all the creatures He has made. Thus the history of his terrible experiment of rebellion was to be a perpetual safeguard to all holy intelligences, to prevent them from being deceived as to the nature of transgression, to save them from committing sin, and suffering its punishment. [38]

As we have seen, God's Word sets forth the role of the Devil in the origin of evil and sin— a most logical and plausible explanation. But some people do not believe that there is any such thing as "the Devil." Their alternative explanations for evil, sin and suffering leave people without hope or recourse, having to blame God, themselves, their mothers, society or cruel cosmic chance.

We find the biblical evidence for the existence of the Devil completely compelling. Moreover, the evidence of evil in the world around us points to a sinister intelligence behind all the misery and suffering we see. Concerning this, E. W. Kenyon wrote:

---

38. White, *Final War*, page 2.

There is no explanation for the intelligence and organization that is behind the power of sin, if there be no such a being as Satan. The prevalence, power and malignity of sin compel us to look for a cause. [39]

E.G. White's perspective is also pertinent here:

While men are ignorant of his devices, this vigilant foe is upon their track every moment. He is intruding his presence in every department of the household, in every street of our cities, in the churches, in the national councils, in the courts of justice, perplexing, deceiving, seducing, everywhere ruining the souls and bodies of men, women, and children, breaking up families, sowing hatred, emulation, strife, sedition, murder. And the Christian world seems to regard these things as though God had appointed them and they must exist. [40]

The sin of Lucifer is most surely the root cause of all evil and suffering, but it is not the only cause. In order to answer the question asked of Jesus in John 9, "Who sinned?" we must look further in God's Word.

The First Adam

God created angels with a purpose, but *man* was His ultimate goal— a family of sons and daughters upon whom He could pour out all the riches of His love. Again He faced the same decision that He did when He created angels: whether or not to create sentient, self-conscious beings capable of independent moral and intellectual judgment. Central to this independence would be the capacity to both accept and reciprocate His love.

As long as God had created only animals in whom is merely instinctual knowledge, no evil was possible. But these creatures were incapable of sharing with and appreciating all that God is and has done. They were trapped in a very limited view of the world and were not able to worship God or recognize Him as their Creator or

---

39. E.W. Kenyon, *The Father And His Family* (Kenyon's Gospel Publishing Society, Seattle WA, 1964), page 57.

40. White, *Final War*, page 17.

source of supply. To be aware of God, a creature would have to be made self-aware first, even though self-awareness could result in self-centeredness instead of appreciation of the Creator (God-awareness).

Was it possible for God to create beings capable of independent moral and intellectual judgment but incapable of choosing anything other than the will of their Creator? No, such beings would be mere robots, preprogrammed to obey. Their obedience or worship would be hollow. Such a Creator would hardly be showing great generosity, or the willingness to risk being unloved or misunderstood. Again, it meant so much to God to love and be loved that He risked being disobeyed and hated. Thus He created the first man, Adam, and the first woman, Eve.

God formed Adam's body from the dust of the ground and then animated his body with physical life, called "soul" (Genesis 2:7). Because God is holy (Isaiah 6:3), and God is spirit (John 4:24), we believe that He created within Adam and Eve holy spirit, His own divine nature. It was holy spirit that made man complete and it was holy spirit that enabled man to have authority and dominion over the earth (Genesis 1:28). Psalm 8 further illustrates Adam's original dominion over the earth.

Psalm 8:3-9

When I consider your heavens, the work of your fingers, the moon and the stars, which you have set in place,

What is man that you are mindful of him, the son of man that you care for him?

You made him a little lower than the heavenly beings [angels] and crowned him with glory and honor.

You made him ruler over the works of your hands; you put everything under his feet:

All flocks and herds, and the beasts of the field,

The birds of the air, and the fish of the sea, all that swim the paths of the seas.

O Lord, our Lord, how majestic is your name in all the earth!

The holy spirit of God within Adam and Eve was their key to exercising their God-given dominion over creation. Without it, they would be no match for the spirit-being "Satan." It is not difficult to imagine the fallen Lucifer seething with rage against the God who had expelled him from heaven. With the creation of man, this evil being saw his opportunity to get back at God, and he hatched a plot to do so.

Man's Original Sin

It is pertinent at this point to discuss how it was that Satan deceived Eve and influenced Adam to willfully disobey God, because Satan continues to this day to use a similar ploy to turn men from the One True God.

Genesis 3:1 (KJV)

Now the serpent was more subtil than any beast of the field which the Lord God had made. And he said unto the woman, Yea, hath God said, Ye shall not eat of every tree of the garden?

In essence, Satan said to Eve: "Are you serious? God won't let you enjoy *all* the fruits of the garden? Why not? That's a little unfair, don't you think? Are you sure He really has your best interests at heart, or is He just keeping something good away from you for His own benefit?" Please note that *the first time the Devil ever spoke to a human being, he assaulted the goodness of God and the veracity of His Word.*

Genesis 3:2,3

The woman said to the serpent, "We may eat fruit from the trees in the garden,

But God did say, 'You must not eat fruit from the tree that is in the middle of the garden, and you must not touch it, or you will die.'"

It would have been nice for Eve to have replied, "Who cares about that *one* tree? Look at all the rest we can enjoy!" But in verse two, she apparently begins to buy into Satan's line of reasoning, as evidenced by her omission of the word "freely," a word that expressed God's lavish provision for them. She then goes on (vs. 3) to add the restrictive phrase "and you must not touch it," which God had never said.

Eve's response (subtracting from and adding to God's Word) is in direct contrast to what Jesus Christ's response would later be each time He was tempted by the same Devil: "It is written!" Jesus Christ stood firmly on the written Word of God. Once Satan knew that the words of God were not going to be Eve's standard for truth, he knew he could sell her on anything that sounded appealing to her. So it is today. If Christians do not adhere diligently to exactly what the written Word of God says, they are susceptible to any idea or theory that sounds remotely plausible.

Genesis 3:4,5

"You will not surely die," the serpent said to the woman.

"For God knows that when you eat of it your eyes will be opened, and you will be like God, knowing good and evil."

In essence, Satan told Eve that God didn't really want heart-to-heart fellowship with her, but instead wanted to keep her under His thumb. Satan said that disobedience to an "unfair" regulation was a good idea, and was in fact the key to real life. He promised that her disobedience would get for her what God refused to give her—an exalted state of consciousness. But the "promise" of Satan was a lie, and resulted in the ruin of Adam and Eve and their progeny.

E.G. White's thoughts on this matter are pertinent:

In his dealing with sin, God could employ only righteousness and truth. Satan could use what God could not—flattery and deceit...to falsify the word of God...claiming that God was not just in laying laws and rules upon the inhabitants of Heaven; that in requiring submission and obedience from His creatures, He was seeking merely the exaltation of Himself. [41]

By the same misrepresentation of the character of God,...causing Him to be regarded as severe and tyrannical, Satan induced man to sin. And having succeeded thus far, he declared that God's unjust restrictions had led to man's fall, as they had led to his own rebellion. [42]

It is painfully obvious that Satan's original deception succeeded all too well.

---

41. *Ibid.*, pages 6, 7.

42. *Ibid.*, page 9.

Romans 5:12 -14

Therefore, just as sin entered the world through one man [Adam], and death through sin, and in this way death came to all men, because all sinned—

For before the law was given, sin was in the world. But sin is not taken into account when there is no law.

Nevertheless, death reigned from the time of Adam to the time of Moses, even over those who did not sin by breaking a command, as did Adam, who was a pattern of the one to come.

"[Sin and] death came into the world as the result of Adam's choice of the god-like knowledge of good and evil over the knowledge of God Himself, which led to his alienation from God, the source of life." [43]   Adam's transgression also transferred man's original dominion and authority over the earth to Satan, as is clear from his offer to Jesus while tempting Him in the wilderness:

Luke 4:5,6

The devil led him up to a high place and showed him in an instant all the kingdoms of the world.

And he said to him, "I will give you all their authority and splendor, for IT HAS BEEN GIVEN TO ME, and I can give it to anyone I want to."

The Devil offered Jesus power over the world, and he was able to make this offer, because, as he said, this power *had been given to him*. By whom? By the one who originally had it— Adam. God had given Adam and Eve dominion over the world, and they had relinquished that dominion to the Devil. [44]

Satan, who certainly had within himself the *ability*, thus acquired from Adam the *legal authority* to ruin God's creation.

---

43. Robert Hach, "Christianity: Persuasion or Coercion" *(Reflections of a Generic Christian*, No. 3, 1992).

44. That is why the Bible refers to Satan as "the god of this age" (II Corinthians 4:4), and warns us of his power: "Finally, be strong in the Lord and in his mighty power. Put on the full armor of God so that you can take your stand against the devil's schemes. For our struggle is not against flesh and blood, but against the ruler, against the authorities, against the powers of this dark world and against the spiritual forces of evil in the heavenly realms" (Ephesians 6:10,11).

Scripture tells us to be self-controlled and alert, because our enemy, the Devil, "prowls around like a roaring lion looking for someone to devour" (I Peter 5:8).

Most people are unaware that Satan continues to deceive humanity with the same basic lies he told Adam and Eve— that God is *not* all love, all light, all good toward man, and that He whimsically afflicts both believers and unbelievers alike. As if that were not bad enough, Satan has promoted the corresponding lie that God also will forever torment in flames all who don't like the way He is and turn away from Him. [45] How could such a hideous thing possibly be done by a loving and righteous God?

In his famous essay, "Why I Am Not A Christian," Bertrand Russell points to the traditional teaching on "hell" as a principal reason for his rejection of the Bible.

> I do not feel that any person who is really and profoundly humane can believe in everlasting punishment...I must say that I think all this doctrine, that hell-fire is a punishment for sin, is a doctrine of cruelty. It is a doctrine that put cruelty into the world and gave the world generations of cruel torture...[46]

We agree with Lord Russell that it is difficult to reconcile a loving God with the notion of eternal torture for sinners, as has been traditionally understood. This doctrine contradicts Ezekiel 18:23,32 and 33:11, which make it clear that God takes no pleasure in the death of the wicked, much less in sadistically tormenting them for eternity.

Perhaps had Russell been taught the truth that there is no such thing in the Bible as "eternal torment," he might have been more able to love its Author.

Satan knows that each man's love for God, and his corresponding trust in Him, is directly proportional to his understanding of God's love for him. This is why he is so relentless in impugning God's love for mankind.

---

45. The truth that there is no such thing in Scripture as "eternal torment" is explained in the CES book *Is There Death After Life?* and even more thoroughly in *The Fire That Consumes,* by Edward Fudge (Providential Press, Houston TX, 1982). One surprising truth made clear in these works is that *fire is not a preservative.*

46. Bertrand Russell, *Unpopular Essays,* "Why I Am Not A Christian" (Simon & Schuster, New York NY, 1950), pages 593,594.

Although some of E.G. White's theology differs considerably from our own, we are glad to set forth whatever she (or anyone else) has written that we believe is biblically accurate and enlightening on a particular subject. She aptly describes how Satan portrays God as the real source of evil:

> Thus the arch-fiend clothes with his own attributes the Creator and Benefactor of mankind. Cruelty is Satanic. God is love; and all that He created was pure, holy, and lovely, until sin was brought in by the first great rebel. Satan himself is the enemy who tempts man to sin, and then destroys him if he can; and when he has made sure of his victim, then he exults in the ruin he has wrought. If permitted, he would sweep the entire race into his net. Were it not for the interposition of divine power, not one son or daughter of Adam would escape.

> He is seeking to overcome men today, as he overcame our first parents, by shaking their confidence in their Creator, and leading them to doubt the wisdom of His government and the justice of His laws. Satan and his emissaries represent God as even worse than themselves, in order to justify their own malignity and rebellion. The great deceiver endeavors to shift his own horrible cruelty of character upon our heavenly Father, that he may cause himself to appear as one greatly wronged by his expulsion from Heaven because he would not submit to so unjust a governor. He presents before the world the liberty which they may enjoy under his mild sway, in contrast with the bondage imposed by the stern decrees of Jehovah. Thus he succeeds in luring souls away from their allegiance to God. [47]

Why does God "allow" Satan's evil activities? Because He cannot act in opposition to His own nature. God is righteous, which means, among other things, that His actions, totally consistent with His internal nature, are ruled by law and not by whim. E.W. Bullinger defines the word "righteous" as "the perfect agreement subsisting between His nature and His acts." [48] This means that God is bound by His nature and by His Word to respect even His

---

47. White, *Final War*, page 79.

48. E.W. Bullinger, *A Critical Lexicon and Concordance to the English and Greek New Testament*, (Samuel Bagster and Sons Ltd., London, Tenth Edition, 1971), page 647.

arch-enemy's legal rights. This is why the Devil can prowl around the earth (Job 1:7), and why he has the legal right to steal, kill and destroy those not redeemed from his power through their faith in Jesus Christ. *How ironic that Satan attributes unfairness to God when it is only God's fairness that allows him to exist.*

E.W. Kenyon speaks pertinently as to the vitally important legal aspect of this spiritual problem:

> There can be no plan of redemption nor theological system that does not recognize Satanic dominion. There can be no excuse for God, if this dominion is not a legal dominion; for if God has a legal right to dispossess the Devil, and put him out of dominion and does not do it, He necessarily becomes guilty of all the acts of the Devil. [49]

Here we have arrived at what is perhaps the crux of the whole issue dealt with in this book: **God does not lack the power or the desire to help people, but He cannot violate His purely righteous nature by overstepping the legal bounds He Himself has determined**. Since the tragic day that Adam delivered the dominion of the world to Satan, God has been making the best of a bad situation, while patiently working toward its total solution and the realization of His original goal of a family living happily ever after. Scripture makes it plain that God will end Satan's dominion in a manner consistent with His righteous nature and His desire for as many people as possible to be saved.

Because God gave to mankind freedom of will, He works with us by persuasion rather than coercion. His goal is, by sound arguments and reasoning, to influence the mind of each human being to the degree that each individual loves, trusts and obeys Him. In regard to God's use of persuasion because of His respect for human dignity, Robert Hach writes:

> That God allows human beings to destroy themselves and one another on a daily basis...is testimony to his respect for human freedom; he refuses to impose "martial law" on a world that is out of control...To assert that God deals with humanity in a rational way, that is, by persuasion, is simply to say that God respects human freedom and dignity, a freedom and dignity that reflect his own image. Freedom is the responsibility of self-government, and persuasion seeks

49. Kenyon, *The Father and His Family*, page 58.

to bring about freely chosen, or autonomous, action on the part of individuals...God, through the biblical message, reasons with those whom he has created in his own image, seeking to change their minds from falsehood to truth, and their hearts from unbelief to faith. Persuasion is the highest order of interpersonal relations, suitable only for humanity in its maturest form. [50]

We have seen how Adam's disobedience to God caused all men born into this world to be subject to the assaults of the prince of darkness and to the problems of sin and death. Adam's original sin led to an entire race tainted by an inherent sin nature and doomed to death. Sickness is actually "death" in part. Now we can answer the question that Jesus' disciples asked in John 9. Why *was* the man born blind? *Sin.* His own? No. His parents? No. Whose? Lucifer's and Adam's.

How could Adam have sinned if he was originally made perfect? The answer is that although God made Adam physically perfect, He did not make him *morally* perfect. That is, Adam was not a moral robot. God gave him the alternative to disobey, and therefore Adam had a real choice between right and wrong. He could choose to do right or to do wrong. God did make Adam and Eve morally *innocent*, which means that they originally had no experiential knowledge of sin or its consequences.

Often it is the case that innocent people are led into sin by evil influences, and it is easy to understand how this happens. This makes the sin of Satan even more contemptible, because *he* had no outside evil influence. He became prideful from within his own being and disobeyed God on his own accord. And so it is clear that God bears absolutely *no* responsibility for the sin of Lucifer, or that of Adam. Indeed, He had anticipated the possibility of their failure and conceived of the ultimate "contingency plan" He would implement for man's redemption from sin. As E.G. White states:

> In the banishment of Satan from Heaven, God declared His justice, and maintained the honor of His throne. But when man had sinned through yielding to the deceptions of this apostate spirit, God gave an evidence of His love by yielding up His only begotten Son to die for the fallen race. In the atonement, the character of God is revealed. The mighty

---

50. Hach, "Christianity: Persuasion or Coercion?", pages 3, 4.

argument of the cross demonstrates to the whole universe that the course of sin which Lucifer had chosen was in nowise chargeable upon the government of God. [51]

Through deception, the Devil tricked Eve into sin. Adam was not deceived (I Timothy 2:14), but disobeyed God by his own free will, and as we saw in Romans 5:12 it is he, not Eve, whom God holds accountable for man's original sin. Remember that Lucifer sinned before Adam did, so Adam's sin was not actually *the* "original sin."

Despite man's sin, God refused to abandon him. In fact, He continues to pursue mankind relentlessly. We will see that the gift of His Son is "God's great assurance that we are not alone." [52] It also shows us that "God's characteristic response to human difficulty is to enter fully into our experience and offer us the comfort of His understanding and companionship." [53] God truly *is* love.

Sin And The Corruption Of God's Creation

Adam sinned, and because of his action, sin and death has infected all his offspring to this day. When Adam and Eve disobeyed God, their death was certain. On the day they sinned, they obviously did not die physically, for they lived many years after that. Rather, they lost their perfect connection to the Creator, the seeds of physical death were planted in them, and their corrupted human nature would dominate them throughout their lives until they died physically. [54] Also, their disobedience brought other grievous consequences upon them and all their descendants.

Genesis 3:16-19

To the woman he said, "I will greatly increase your pains in childbearing; with pain you will give birth to children. Your desire will be for your husband, and he will rule over you."

---

51. White, *Final War*, page 9.

52. Rice, *When Bad Things Happen to God's People*, page 37.

53. *Ibid.*, page 36.

54. Mark Graeser, John Lynn and John Schoenheit, *Is There Death After Life* (Christian Educational Services, Indianapolis IN), page 29.

To Adam he said, "Because you listened to your wife and ate from the tree about which I commanded you, 'You must not eat of it,' Cursed is the ground because of you; through painful toil you will eat of it all the days of your life.

It will produce thorns and thistles for you, and you will eat the plants of the field.

By the sweat of your brow you will eat your food until you return to the ground, since from it you were taken; for dust you are and to dust you will return."

These verses show that *sin* is the root cause of all of mankind's subsequent suffering. It is important to realize that one reason suffering is a part of life is that *the inherent nature* of all things has been corrupted. The original garden of Eden ("Eden" means "delight" or "pleasure") had no thorns, thistles or dangerous animals. For example, one aspect of the "cursed ground" that God spoke to Adam about is that while the earth does not naturally produce wonderful fruits and vegetables, "thorns and thistles" grow naturally in abundance.

These consequences will plague mankind until "the last Adam" completes the perfect restoration of creation. Because of Adam's sin and Satan's subsequent dominion over the earth, suffering is a part of life, and will be until sin and death are no more (Revelation 21:4). Furthermore, when the Lord rules the earth in His millenial kingdom, there will again be an abundance of food, no dangerous animals, no war, perfect justice, and the earth will again be a delightful place. The curse on the earth, with all its ramifications, will be totally removed when God finally creates a new heaven and a new earth for all the righteous (Revelation 22:3).

Romans 8:19-22

The creation waits in eager expectation for the sons of God to be revealed.

For the creation was subjected to frustration, not by its own choice, but by the will of the one [Satan] who subjected it, in hope

That the creation itself will be liberated from its bondage to decay and brought into the glorious freedom of the children of God.

We know that the whole creation has been groaning as in the pains of childbirth right up to the present time.

We hope that the following analogy will help illustrate the corruption of creation, that is, the overall corruption of all forms of life, related to and determined by the advent of sin into the world. Suppose your local convenience store had a "Win The Mona Lisa" contest. Suppose you won. Imagine your friends gathered around as you unwrap it in your living room. "What an awesome master-piece!" "Look at that gorgeous creation!" "That Leonardo guy was amazing!"

Just then your young son spills a pitcher of raspberry juice on the painting. Try as you will, you cannot remove the stain. "Oh, no! But hey, it's still the Mona Lisa, and it's the only painting we have, let's hang it up." When people looked at it, what would they see? They would clearly see that it was once an exquisite masterpiece done by an incredible artist, but they would also plainly see that it has been indelibly marred. There is only one solution to this problem, and that is for the original artist to re-create a similar masterpiece. That is exactly what God, through Jesus Christ, will do. He will create a new earth for all who have believed in Him.

At this time we have no choice but to live amidst a corrupted creation. "A rose by any other name is still a rose." True, but now it has *thorns*! "This is for you, darling." "Ouch!" As we saw, thorns came into being after man's original sin. Satan, who already had the ability, had gotten the authority to alter the genetic structure in a rose. We believe that in Genesis 3:18, "thorns and thistles" are representa-tive of all corruption due to Adam's sin.

You're holding a beautiful little baby boy, and you marvel at his physical symmetry, his intricacy, his precision and his potential versatility. What a masterpiece! Then he throws up on you. You bask in 70 degree, low-humidity sunshine on the deck of your oceanside home. Fleecy clouds drift by and a soft breeze caresses you. What a glorious day! Then the breeze becomes a hurricane and your oceanside home is six inches high. Why? The corruption of creation.

Scripture makes it obvious that when God originally created the world, He anticipated the possibility of its ruin, and planned for its necessary restoration. As we will see in the next chapter, this plan is still in the process of being fulfilled through Jesus Christ, the last Adam.

CHAPTER 3

JESUS CHRIST IS THE SOLUTION

God: Consistent With His Nature

In regard to putting evil, sin and suffering in proper perspective, it is crucial to understand that God cannot do anything contrary to His own nature.

Romans 3:8

Why not say— as we are being slanderously reported as saying and as some claim that we say— "Let us do evil that good may result"? Their condemnation is deserved.

For God, the righteous end He will bring to pass cannot justify any unrighteous means. He will *never* do evil so that good may come. So the next time you hear a Christian who has been afflicted by some sickness or tragedy tell how this was God's way of testing him, reproving him or helping him grow in faith, you can tell him the truth that it was not God Who afflicted him, and that God is still with him to help him. Who knows? That might be the catalyst for his faith to grow to the point where he receives supernatural deliverance.

You could even share with the person what God Himself says about whether or not He tests people with tragedy:

James 1:13 and 17

When tempted, no one should say, "God is tempting me." For God cannot be tempted by evil, nor does he tempt anyone;

Every good and perfect gift is from above, coming down from the Father of the heavenly lights, who does not change like shifting shadows.

It could be asked why God did not just squash Adam right after he sinned. Another good question. The answer is multi-faceted. At its root is the truth that God can only act in ways consistent with His nature, which is love. Also, He had committed Himself to the plan of mankind living here upon the earth. Had He destroyed Adam, this plan would have come to nought. Within Adam was the Christ-plan God had held in reserve to restore mankind.

We believe that E.G. White's previously expressed logic (see Chapter Two) as to why God did not destroy the Devil right after he originally sinned is pertinent to Adam and his descendants also. In His love and justice, God allows each person to decide for himself whether or not to obey Him, and whether to receive the benefits of obedience or suffer the consequences of disobedience. By clearly showing mankind the stark contrast between the results of godliness and the results of sinfulness, and by allowing sin's consequences to be fully manifested over the course of human history, God will have finally demonstrated to all men His goodness, love, righteousness and the wisdom of total obedience to Him.

By the way, it *is* available for people (like you) to recognize God's goodness in their lifetimes and join His family by being "born again" as millions have done. One's first birth did not guarantee him everlasting life. One's new birth as a son of God does just that.

To be born into the family of God, one must confess Jesus Christ as his Lord, and believe that God raised Him from the dead (Romans 10:9,10). The more one understands who Jesus Christ is, what He accomplished for God during His life on earth and what He is doing now as the exalted Lord, the more appealing it is to trust in Him and walk with Him. Let us therefore begin with the first verse in the Bible that refers to Jesus Christ.

The Plan: Another Adam

In Genesis 3:15, right after the "original sin," God announced His plan to solve the two-fold problem of sin and death: another "Adam," who would someday rectify all that the first Adam ruined.

Genesis 3:15

And I will put enmity between you and the woman, and between your offspring [seed] and hers; he will crush your head, and you will strike his heel.

"Seed" implies birth— the only way by which all human beings could begin life since Adam and Eve.   In the act of conception, the seed comes from the male. The fact that Genesis 3:15 says "her" seed indicates that it was to be a virgin to whom the promised "seed" would be born, and that the seed would be implanted in her womb by God Himself. We today know that the Man called Jesus Christ is the one spoken of in Genesis 3:15. [55]

I Corinthians 15:45 refers to Jesus as the "last Adam." To be the last Adam, Jesus Christ had to be a man like the first Adam. To be the perfect sacrifice for man, Jesus had to be a human being—a "lamb from out of the flock," but without spot or blemish. It was God who made Jesus physically perfect. How? By creating a perfect "Seed" in the womb of a virgin. Thus Jesus was a human being like the first Adam, but without the sinful nature all other humans have inherited from him. God gave Jesus every human quality necessary for Him to fulfill God's purpose for His life, but it was up to Jesus to do it.

Had Jesus Christ been a moral robot, He could not possibly have sinned. If He could not have sinned, He could not *genuinely* have been tempted in all ways as we are (Hebrews 4:15). Had He not genuinely been tempted, and had He not overcome temptation by trust in and obedience to the Word of God, Jesus would not now be able to help us in our temptation, as He most certainly is. Hebrews 2:18 states: "Because he himself suffered when he was tempted, he is able to help those who are being tempted."

Like the first Adam, the last Adam— Jesus Christ— began his life physically and mentally perfect, but not morally perfect. Rather,

---

55. *Jesus Christ, The Diameter of the Ages* (CES Bi-Monthly Tapes, Apr/May—Nov/Dec 1990) and *A New Race For a New Age* (CES Bi-Monthly Tape, Nov/Dec 1992).

He too was morally innocent. Because of His sinless nature *and* a lifetime of total obedience to God His Father, even unto the death of the cross (Philippians 2:8), Jesus was the only man who could have been the perfect sacrifice for man's sin. By His one righteous act of going to the cross, Jesus legally fulfilled the requirements of God's justice and actually *earned* the righteousness that the first Adam was *given* and then lost.

Romans 5:15-17

But the gift is not like the trespass. For if the many died by the trespass of the one man [Adam], how much more did God's grace and the gift that came by the grace of the one man, Jesus Christ, overflow to the many!

Again, the gift of God is not like the result of the one man's [Adam's] sin: The judgment followed one sin and brought condemnation, but the gift followed many trespasses and brought justification.

For if, by the trespass of the one man [Adam], death reigned through that one man, how much more will those who receive God's abundant provision of grace and of the gift of righteousness reign in life through the one man, Jesus Christ.

Why Did Jesus Have To Suffer And Die?

Two primary qualities of God help us understand why Jesus Christ had to suffer and die in order to redeem mankind. First, God is righteous. Thus His justice demands that a penalty for sin be paid. As Kenyon writes:

God cannot ignore the fact of man's hideous transgression. That transgression must be punished, and if man is restored to God, it must be upon grounds that will not pauperize man nor rob him of his self respect; but it must be upon legal grounds that will perfectly justify man in the sight of God... [56]

Second, God is love. Thus, in His grace and mercy, He decreed that the penalty for sin could be paid by a substitute, providing that

---

56. Kenyon, *The Father and His Family*, page 115.

the substitute be sinless. God wanted, and mankind needed, a man who:

> ...met the demands, first, of the heart of Deity for a perfect human who would do His will; second, He met the demands of fallen man in that as a man He met the Devil and conquered him in honorable open combat. [57]

Because of the magnitude of Adam's sin and its reverberating ramifications, only the death penalty would satisfy true justice. Hebrews 9:22 says that "without the shedding of blood there is no forgiveness [of sin]." In the Old Testament, it was the death of unblemished "stand-in" lambs and other animals that God allowed to temporarily cover His people's sins (Hebrews 10:1-14). These sacrifices were foreshadows, or types, of the coming Redeemer, Jesus Christ. He is the true "Lamb of God" whose blood was shed to take away the sin of the world (John 1:29).

Hebrews 9:14

> How much more, then, will the blood of Christ, who through the eternal Spirit offered himself unblemished to God, cleanse our consciences from acts that lead to death, so that we may serve the living God!

As we have stated, Jesus Christ was the only man who was "without spot or blemish," both genetically and behaviorally. As such, only He could qualify to offer His life as the payment for the sin and sins of mankind. The suffering and death of Jesus Christ was part of God's plan to make available salvation to all mankind.

Hebrews 9:27,28

> Just as man is destined to die once, and after that to face judgment,

> So Christ was sacrificed once to take away the sins of many people; and he will appear a second time, not to bear sin, but to bring salvation to those who are waiting for him.

What the blood of bulls and goats could do only temporarily for Israel in the Old Testament, the blood of Jesus has done once and for all for everyone who believes in Him. He bore our sins in his own body on the cross (I Peter 2:24). By His freedom of will He gave up

---

57. *Ibid.*, page 192.

His life for us. He willingly endured the pain of the cross and death for all men. We must understand, however, that it was not God who was responsible for Jesus' death. Note the following verses:

I Corinthians 2:7,8:

No, we speak of God's secret wisdom, a wisdom that has been hidden and that God destined for our glory before time began.

None of the rulers of this age understood it, for if they had, they would not have crucified the Lord of glory.

The "rulers of this age" are Satan and his evil-spirit sidekicks (the disobedient angels that were cast down to earth with him). God's Word plainly says that it is the Devil who was responsible for killing Jesus Christ.

Once the dominion of the world was given to Satan, and mankind was ruined by sin, God has had to ask people to step into harm's way so that His redemptive purposes could be accomplished. Jesus Christ is the chief example of this, and there are many others (see Hebrews 11). Jesus suffered so that those who believe on Him can one day have peace and joy forever, and a taste of it even in this life. In Jesus, we see the epitome of the redemptive value of suffering, a subject we will discuss later.

Hebrews 5:7-9 (Moffatt)

In the days of his flesh, with bitter cries and tears, he offered prayers and supplications to Him who was able to save him from death; and he was heard, because of his godly fear. Thus, Son though he was, he learned by all he suffered how to obey, and by being THUS PERFECTED he became the source of eternal salvation for all who obey him, being designated by God high priest *with the rank of Melchizedek.*

We feel the Moffatt translation (e.g.,"thus perfected") best represents the truth of the Greek text that Jesus attained moral perfection through suffering and death. It was God who totally "perfected" Jesus by raising Him from the dead with a glorious new body and exalting Him as Lord, as the following verses make clear:

Hebrews 2:9-11

But we see Jesus, who was made a little lower than the angels, now crowned with glory and honor because he suffered death, so that by the grace of God he might taste death for everyone.

In bringing many sons to glory, it was fitting that God, for whom and through whom everything exists, should make the author of their salvation perfect through suffering.

Both the one who makes men holy and those who are made holy are of the same family. So Jesus is not ashamed to call them brothers.

Jesus Christ is the last Adam, the fulfillment of God's prophecy in Genesis 3:15. As our Redeemer, Jesus purchased our salvation with His own blood. He provided, and is, the way back to God that Adam had lost. Those who confess Him as Lord and believe in His resurrection are saved, fully equipped to live in this corrupted world and guaranteed ultimate and everlasting victory over sin and death, as we shall see.

All's Well That Ends Well

For us to adequately deal with suffering, it is imperative that we not only know its source, but also have an assurance of its coming to an end. As Richard Rice writes:

In order to respond courageously to suffering, we need to know more than simply God's past and present relation to it. We need to know what He is going to do about it and its ultimate disposition in the future...God remains committed to His purposes for human history. Consequently, good is ultimately more powerful than evil, and life is fundamentally worth living. [58]

As we have seen, God gave man freedom of will, and thus allowed for the possibility of sin. God knew that sin's dominance would be *temporary* and that He could and would one day bring about a permanent and glorious solution. In the meantime, He did not want to run a big *puppet show*, yet unfortunately that is exactly how much of "fundamental" Christianity represents life, as we will see later on in this book.

---

58. Rice, *When Bad Things Happen to God's People*, pages 39 and 51.

Remember, God is righteous—that is, He is fair, just, and legally honest to all His creation. He can do nothing that would contradict His own nature. *Justice is impossible without judgment*, which God, through Christ, will ultimately render. In regard to this final judgment of sin and evil, E.G. White waxes eloquent:

> In the final execution of the Judgment it will be seen that no cause [no justification] for sin exists. When the Judge of all the earth shall demand of Satan, "Why hast thou rebelled against Me, and robbed Me of the subjects of My kingdom?" the originator of evil can render no excuse. Every mouth will be stopped, and all the hosts of rebellion will be speechless.
>
> The cross of Calvary, while it declares the law immutable, proclaims to the universe that the wages of sin is death. In the Saviour's expiring cry, "It is finished," the death-knell of Satan was rung. The great controversy which had been so long in progress was then decided, and the final eradication of evil was made certain. The Son of God passed through the portals of the tomb, that "through death He might destroy him that had the power of death, that is, the devil" (Hebrews 2:14). Lucifer's desire for self-exaltation had led him to say, "I will exalt my throne above the stars of God.... I will be like the Most High." God declares, "I will bring thee to ashes upon the earth,...and never shall thou be any more" (Isaiah 14:13; Ezekiel 28:18,19). When "the day cometh that shall burn as an oven; and all the proud, yea, and all that do wickedly, shall be stubble: and the day that cometh shall burn them up, saith the Lord of hosts, that it shall leave them neither root nor branch." (Malachi 4:1)
>
> The whole universe will have become witnesses to the nature and results of sin. And its utter extermination, which in the beginning would have brought fear to angels and dishonor to God, will now vindicate His love and establish His honor before a universe of beings who delight to do His will, and in whose heart is His law. Never will evil again be manifest... The law of God, which Satan reproached as the yoke of bondage, will be honored as the law of liberty. A tested and proved creation will never again be turned from allegiance to Him whose character has been fully manifested before them as fathomless love and infinite wisdom. [59]

---

59. White, *Final War*, pages 12-13.

God's Word makes it clear that until that glorious day when sin and its consequences are forever eradicated, He is willing to take the long way around to a righteous conclusion so that as many people as possible can come to repentance. His loving nature prohibits any other course of action. Consider the following verses:

II Peter 3:9

The Lord is not slow in keeping his promise, as some understand slowness. He is patient with you, not wanting anyone to perish, but everyone to come to repentance.

I Timothy 2:3,4

This is good, and pleases God our Saviour,

Who wants all men to be saved and to come to a knowledge of the truth.

Ezekiel 33:11 (KJV)

Say to them, *As* I live, saith the Lord God, I have no pleasure in the death of the wicked; but that the wicked turn from his way and live: turn ye, turn ye from your evil ways; for why will ye die, O house of Israel?

Deuteronomy 30:19

This day I call heaven and earth as witnesses against you that I have set before you life and death, blessings and curses. Now choose life, so that you and your children may live.

Although not all men will respond affirmatively to God's offer of salvation, His Word makes it clear that He earnestly desires that they do, and that He gives them every possible opportunity. Sometimes people may ask, "Why doesn't God once and for all put a stop to the suffering?" If the questioner is one who has thus far rejected God's Word, the answer is, "He will, but if He did it *now*, you would be 'history!' So believe in the Lord Jesus Christ and get born again, and you will instead be a part of "His-story."

If you intend to read an Agatha Christie novel, do not start by reading the last chapter— it will ruin the whole book. But the Bible is different. Knowing the "last chapter" is what makes the whole book so fabulous. *WE WIN!!!* The last Adam will exercise His earned dominion to crush Satan's head and rescue us from this present evil age. In regard to our hope of glory, Richard Rice writes:

If God is ultimately in charge of things and if suffering was never meant to be, there must come a time when suffering will be a thing of the past. Without this future dimension, every response to suffering falls short. It fails to give us a basis for personal hope.

We have seen that suffering not only involves physical pain. It also threatens the meaning of existence. It hinders or prevents the fulfillment of our plans and dreams. It keeps us from living our lives to the fullest. Unless there is a future beyond suffering, and unless we can participate in it personally, suffering has the last word. [60]

Praise God that He has already given us "the last word"— *His Word*! Even the most tragic circumstances will be redeemed, and when our victory is consummated, there will be no more death, sorrow, tears or pain (Revelation 21:4).

---

60. Rice, *When Bad Things Happen To God's People,* page 90.

CHAPTER 4

OLD TESTAMENT OR NEW— WHICH ONE IS TRUE?

Literal or Figurative?

S peaking about the written Word of God, Jesus Christ said, "Thy Word is truth" (John 17:17). When it comes to spiritual things beyond the realm of man's five senses, the Word of God is the *only* credible witness. In stark contrast to the vague, groundless theories and speculations originating in the minds of men, God, the Author of life, presents clear, straightforward answers to man's most pressing questions. Thus we must diligently look into God's Word, the literature of eternity, and let Him speak for Himself about the deep issues of life, such as evil, sin and suffering.

The Bible is the standard of all literature, and God the Author of all authors. As literature, the Word of God contains a rich variety of linguistic thoughts, expressions and usages. Like any author, God has the right to use language as He deems appropriate to His purposes. E.W. Bullinger, an eminent British Bible scholar (1837-1913), identified the use of more than 200 figures of speech in the Bible. These figures greatly enrich its literary value, but more importantly are vital to our understanding and application of God's manual for living.

Each reader of God's Word is entrusted with a certain degree of personal responsibility. Those who endeavor to study, understand and interpret the Bible must become very sensitive to the literary devices it employs, because its study is not merely for cultural amusement. Our very lives, both temporal and eternal, depend on an accurate understanding of God's words, which are the very "words of life."

One's concept of the Bible determines the attitude with which he approaches it. If you think of it as an impersonal "rulebook," you will tend to consult it only in regard to "infractions," rather than be motivated to study it with the intent of establishing a personal relationship with its Author. If you think it is only a history book, you may read it with little more than a detached curiosity.

Some have simplistically attempted to reduce it to a strictly literal document, thus trapping themselves in a maze of contradictions they are forced to ignore or deny. Others have so divorced the words of Scripture from the normal linguistic constraints of grammar, semantics, syntax and logic that the Author's original intent is lost in a fog of personal speculation.

When God makes statements of fact, or uses language in the way it is normally used, we should surely take note. When He departs from customary usage of words, syntax, grammar and statements true to fact, we must take double note, for such departures serve to communicate truth better than can literal statements of fact. How can we tell when a biblical statement is literal or figurative? E.W. Bullinger asks and answers this most pertinent question:

> It may be asked, "How are we to know then, when words are to be taken in their simple, original form (i.e., literally), and when they are to be taken in some other and peculiar form (i.e., as a Figure)? The answer is that, *whenever and wherever it is possible, the words of Scripture are to be understood literally, but when a statement appears to be contrary to our experience, or*

to known fact, or revealed truth; or seems to be at variance with the
general teaching of the Scriptures, then we may reasonably expect
that some figure is employed [Emphasis ours].   And as it is
employed only to call our attention to some specially designed emphasis, we are at once bound to diligently examine
the figure for the purpose of discovering and learning the
truth that is thus emphasized. [61]

One can easily see how critical a knowledge of figures of speech
is to understanding God's written communication to man. Without
such knowledge, the honest reader comes face to face with over-
whelming contradictions that, if not resolved, cannot but undermine
his confidence that the Scriptures are truly "God-breathed." It is our
contention that Scripture being the Word of *God* presupposes its
inherent accuracy and consistency.   Thus we must explore the
figurative language pertinent to the subject of evil, sin and suffering.

As the only credible witness of eternal and spiritual verities, the
Bible gives testimony in a variety of ways— some literal, some
figurative.   Taking literal statements figuratively and figurative
statements literally is a root cause of major doctrinal error in the
orthodox Christian Church. This has too often resulted in the Word
of God being twisted, distorted and misrepresented. If "God IS love"
(I John 4:8), then He *cannot* do anything that is not loving, and any
verses that seem to indicate that He does cannot be taken literally. As
you will see, understanding the figurative language in God's Word
is vital when it comes to reconciling the truth that God is love with
the problem of evil, sin and suffering.

A Kingdom Divided Against Itself Cannot Stand

In understanding God's dealings with men, we must see that
Jesus Christ is the fulcrum of history. His life, death, resurrection,
ascension and exaltation as Lord changed a number of things relative
to the way in which God dealt with mankind. One thing that did not
change from the Old Testament to the New Testament is that God
never does evil, nor does He send suffering to those who love Him.

---

61. E.W. Bullinger, *Figures Of Speech Used In The Bible* (Baker Book House, Grand
Rapids MI, 1978), page xv.

The New Testament is very clear that the Devil, not God, is the source of evil and of much human suffering. For example, it is the Devil who holds the power of death, which God specifically calls an "enemy" (I Corinthians 15:26).

Hebrews 2:14

Since the children have flesh and blood, he too shared in their humanity so that by his death he might destroy him who holds the power of death— that is, the devil.

The Devil, not God, comes to steal, kill and destroy.

John 10:10

The thief comes only to steal and kill and destroy; I have come that they may have life, and have it to the full.

The Devil oppresses people, but God and His Son do only good.

Acts 10:38

How God anointed Jesus of Nazareth with the Holy Spirit and power, and how he went around doing good and healing all who were under the power of the devil, because God was with him.

Jesus Christ came to destroy the work of the Devil.

I John 3:8

He who does what is sinful is of the devil, because the devil has been sinning from the beginning. The reason the Son of God appeared was to destroy the devil's work.

Please read I John 3:8 again very carefully, because it contains a great truth. There are many Christians who will readily admit that the sickness and death so widespread on the earth today is indeed "the Devil's work." However, many also say, as did John Calvin, that the Devil could not do any of it unless God allowed him to. [62] This

---

62. John Calvin, *Institutes of the Christian Religion, Book 1*, Editor: John T. McNeill (Westminster Press, Philadelphia, PA 1960), Pages 4-7. Calvin wrote, "From himself [Satan] and his own wickedness, therefore, arises his passionate and deliberate opposition to God. By this wickedness he is urged on to attempt courses of action which he believes to be most hostile to God. But because with the bridle of his power God holds him bound and restrained, he carries out only those things which have been divinely permitted to him; and so he obeys his Creator, whether he will or not, because he is compelled to yield him service wherever God impels him." Of course,

turns God into a "godfather," directing criminal activity at His will, and it ignores the first part of I John 3:8, which says the Devil has been sinning from the beginning. If he has been doing the will of God, he has not been "sinning." Only if he is doing things that God does not want him doing can he be said to be "sinning."

A cursory reading of the Bible seems to indicate a big change in God between the Old and New Testaments. This cannot be the case, however, because God does not change (Malachi 3:6). Neither does He ever contradict Himself. Both the Old and New Testaments are "God-breathed" (II Timothy 3:16), and therefore must be perfectly harmonious. Let us now note some things that seem to be contradictions, and then we will show why they are not and how they are biblically reconciled.

The Old Testament seems to make God the cause of disease, destruction and death. The New Testament attributes these things to the Devil. The Old Testament portrays God as the ruler of the world, in charge of both good and evil, and that is what the Hebrew people believed. Job said, "Shall we accept good from God, and not trouble?" (Job 2:10). The New Testament, however, paints a different picture: the Devil is "the god of this age" (II Corinthians 4:4). It is he who controls much of what is going on in the world, it is he who offered all the world's power and glory to Jesus (Matthew 4:8, Luke 4:5,6). In the Old Testament, God is portrayed as the cause of good *and* bad. In the New Testament, the Devil causes evil (John 10:10a), but God sends "every good and perfect gift" (James 1:17).

In the Old Testament, the Hebrew people recognized the existence of a spirit realm. They knew that some spirits did horrible things, but believed they were sent by God to do His work. Thus King Saul's attendants said to him, "See, an evil spirit from God is tormenting you" (I Samuel 16:15). Nowhere is there set forth the

---

there are more than a few Christians who realize the truth that it is Satan, the Devil, God's archenemy, who is responsible for most of the suffering that has plagued mankind since Adam's original sin. But some, like Calvin, argue that Satan is merely playing a scapegoat role assigned to him by God. Others say that Satan must get permission from God before he can afflict people, but this also leaves God ultimately responsible for evil. Still others who acknowledge the existence of Satan teach that a Christian can avoid all suffering by walking in fellowship with God. This in part leads to the corresponding error that one's human mind is in reality the cause of whatever comes upon him, good or bad. It also flatly contradicts God's Word, which states that all those who live a godly life will suffer persecution (II Timothy 3:12).

truth about two spiritual kingdoms at war with each other. Nowhere in the Old Testament is anyone told to cast out an evil spirit. Rather, God told the people of Israel to kill certain people who opposed them. The spiritual battle was manifest in the physical realm. But in the New Testament we clearly see the battle between God's *spiritual* forces and the Devil's army of evil spirits. Rather than kill people, Jesus cast out many of these evil spirits from them. Here are a few examples:

Matthew 8:16

When evening came, many who were demon-possessed were brought to him, and he drove out the spirits with a word and healed all the sick.

Mark 1:34

And Jesus healed many who had various diseases. He also drove out many demons, but he would not let the demons speak because they knew who he was.

Mark 16:9

When Jesus rose early on the first day of the week, he appeared first to Mary Magdalene, out of whom he had driven seven demons.

Luke 11:14,15,17,18

Jesus was driving out a demon that was mute, When the demon left, the man who had been mute spoke, and the crowd was amazed.

But some of them said, "By Beelzebub, the prince of demons, he is driving out demons."

Jesus knew their thoughts and said to them: "Any kingdom divided against itself will be ruined, and a house divided against itself will fall."

If Satan is divided against himself, how can his kingdom stand? I say this because you claim that I drive out demons by Beelzebub.

The above record in Luke is very telling. Some in the crowd accused Jesus of casting out devils with devils. Jesus' answer was that a kingdom divided against itself cannot stand. This logic certainly holds true for God's kingdom also. God is not pitting His own forces against one another. He does not allow a person to become possessed by devils (with all the horrors to one's life, family and friends that can accompany such possession) and then later cast out the devils He allowed in. If He did, and if Jesus' logic is correct, His (God's) kingdom would not stand.

Not only did Jesus Himself cast out evil spirits, but he also equipped his disciples with power over evil spirits.

Mark 3:14,15

He appointed twelve— designating them apostles— that they might be with him

And that he might send them out to preach and to have authority to drive out demons.

Luke 10:17

The seventy-two returned with joy and said, "Lord, even the demons submit to us in your name."

We submit that of all the awesome men and women of God whose exploits are chronicled in the Old Testament, not one of them said anything like the above statement made by the disciples.

Luke 10:18-20

He replied, " I saw Satan fall like lightning from heaven.

I have given you authority to trample on snakes and scorpions and to overcome all the power of the enemy; nothing will harm you.

However, do not rejoice that the spirits submit to you, but rejoice that your names are written in heaven."

Likewise today, Christians are instructed to fight against evil spirits.

Mark 16:17a

And these signs will accompany those who believe: In my name they will drive out demons;

Ephesians 6:12

For our struggle is not against flesh and blood, but against the rulers, against the authorities, against the powers of this dark world and against the spiritual forces of evil in the heavenly realms.

In the book of Acts, the apostles (Acts 5:16), Philip (Acts 8:7) and Paul (Acts 16:16-18) are all specifically mentioned casting out evil spirits. The above sections of Scripture vividly show the contrast between the Old Testament and the New Testament. If evil spirits were really just agents for God acting out His will, then opposing them would be worse than hopeless, it would be sin. Furthermore, the New Testament portrays some evil spirits as having sinned so badly that they are now "in prison" awaiting the judgment (II Peter 2:4). [63] God would have no cause to put these especially evil spirits in prison if they were only able to act with His permission in the first place, would He?

In the Old Testament, God is portrayed as killing both believers and unbelievers. But in the New Testament, Jesus calls the Devil a murderer (John 8:44), and Hebrews 2:14 says that it is the Devil who holds the power of death. Never, never, never in the New Testament is the death of a believer attributed to God.

Jesus Christ Lifted The Veil

A major problem with "orthodox" Christian thinking today is that so many Christians believe what the Old Testament says about God without critically examining their beliefs in light of the New Testament. Is the Old Testament *literally* correct: Does God kill believers? Does God send evil spirits to torment people? Does God cause sickness and disease? The answer to each question is the same: "No, a thousand times no!" The New Testament clarifies for us the truth on these issues, and only in its light can the Old Testament be understood.

John 1:17

For the law was given through Moses; grace and TRUTH [biblically, the Greek word *aletheia* basically means "reality", i.e., things as they really are] came through Jesus Christ.

Jesus Christ brought to light truths that were never known before His lifetime. That is why the Old Testament *must* be read in light of the New Testament.

---

63. *The Sons of God of Genesis Six* (CES Bi-Monthly Tape Jan/Feb 1993).

II Corinthians 3:14b-16

...for to this day the same veil remains when the old covenant is read. It has not been removed, because only in Christ is it taken away.

Even to this day when Moses is read, a veil covers their hearts.

But whenever anyone turns to the Lord, the veil is taken away.

John 1:18 is an interesting verse when considered in light of the New Testament bringing new information that the Old Testament did not have.

John 1:18 (KJV)

No man hath seen God at any time; the only begotten Son, which is in the bosom of the Father, he [Jesus] hath declared him [God].

According to this verse, Jesus Christ "declared" God. The Greek word translated here as "declared" is *exegeomai*, which means "to lead out," "to make known," or "to unfold." Jesus Christ was the first one in history to clearly manifest to mankind the heart of God as a *Father*. The God whom we know as all love, all light and all goodness was made known as never before by His Son Jesus Christ.

It is very, very important to realize that Jesus Christ revealed God in a completely new light that had not been known in the Old Testament. We again quote the following verses from the Gospel of John:

John 1:17,18

For the law was given through Moses; grace and TRUTH came through Jesus Christ.

No man hath seen God at any time; the only begotten Son, which is in the bosom of the Father, he [Jesus] hath declared him [God].

Please note that truth, in its fullness, came not with Moses, but with Jesus Christ. It was He who for the first time in history made God truly understandable. It is not that the Old Testament believers knew nothing of God, but rather that their knowledge and understanding of Him were quite limited ("veiled"). Since truth came by Jesus Christ, we believe that the first part of verse eighteen— "no man hath seen God at anytime"— means that no man had "known" God at any previous time. It is Jesus Christ who reveals, or makes known, God to man.

In many languages, "to see" is a common idiom for "to know." In the Hebrew language, one of the definitions for "see" (Hebrew=*ra'ah*) is "see, so as to learn, to know." [64] Similarly, the Greek word translated "see" in verse 18 (*horao*) can be "to see with the eyes" or "to see with the mind, to perceive, know." [65] Even in English, one of the definitions for "see" is "to know or understand." For example, when two people are discussing something, one might say to the other, "I see what you mean."

The usage of "see" as it pertains to knowing is found in many places in the New Testament. Jesus said to Philip "Anyone who has seen me has seen the Father" (John 14:9). Here again the word "see" is used to indicate knowing. Anyone who *knew* Christ (not just those who "saw" Him) would know the Father. In fact, Christ had made that plain two verses earlier when He said to Philip "If you really knew me, you would know my Father as well" (John 14:7). The reason it is so vital to realize the shift in people's understanding of God that took place because of Christ's teachings is that *any argument that uses Old Testament scriptures to prove that God causes or allows suffering must be examined in light of the New Testament teaching.* Otherwise there will be great confusion.

What we have examined in this chapter are illustrations of the dynamic and progressive revelation of the Word of God. What was understood literally in the Old Testament becomes figurative as further truth is revealed. For example, Moses smote the rock and water came out. From the New Testament we understand that the rock represented Christ, and the water everlasting life (I Corinthians 10:4). Similarly, by deliberately revealing very few facts about Satan in the Old Testament, God caused His people to understand Him as the literal cause of both good and evil. The language pertaining to Satan is ambiguous and laced with figures so that it can be understood in some other sense also (e.g., the King of Tyre, "Lucifer," et al).

---

64. *The New Brown, Driver, and Briggs Hebrew and English Lexicon of the Old Testament* (Francis Brown, Editor, Associated Publishers and Authors, Inc., Lafayette IN, reprinted 1981), page 907.

65. *The New Thayer's Greek-English Lexicon of the New Testament* (Joseph Henry Thayer, Associated Publishers and Authors, Lafayette IN 47903, 1979), page 451.

In light of New Testament revelation, we can go back to the Old Testament and recognize spiritual truths that were not clear at that time. We can recognize the significance of Jesus' resurrection, even though it was only *specifically* mentioned in one phrase in the Old Testament: "Nor will you let your holy one see decay" (Psalm 16:10— quoted in Acts 2:27,31). Now we can also see the resurrection in the Old Testament analogy of Jonah, and in the phrase "this day have I begotten thee" (Psalm 2:7— KJV).

We just saw that, in some cases, what was understood literally in the Old Testament is correctly seen to be figurative as further truth is revealed in the New Testament. What about the converse? Some of what was understood figuratively becomes more literal with further revelation. For instance, "Jesus Christ our Passover" (I Corinthians 5:7) becomes more literal the more we understand the parallels between the Paschal lamb and the "lamb of God"— that He would have died at exactly the same time, etc. Our understanding of the future "wrath of God" as mentioned in the New Testament is made more literal than figurative as we recognize the Old Testament records in which it is literally displayed (Sodom and Gomorrah, etc.).

By seeking to understand the *whole* Word of God, we can learn to recognize the combination of literal and figurative language woven together into a tapestry of truth. Thus we will now consider the key figure of speech relevant to a biblical understanding of God's relation to evil, sin and suffering.

CHAPTER 5

GOD IS GOOD
(WITH FIGURES!)

Meet Mr. Metonymy

There is no question that the Bible is replete with examples of God acting in ways that seem to contradict His loving nature, not to mention offend our sense of decency, justice and common sense. These instances must be carefully analyzed and weighed against the whole of the biblical revelation, as well as compared to all the clear scriptures that reveal God's essential goodness, fairness and love.

Learning is an exciting adventure, especially when what you are learning is fundamental to your relationship with the Creator of the heavens and the earth. In mathematics, knowing calculus allows you to accomplish very beneficial things you cannot do knowing only algebra. Yet algebra is a pre-requisite to geometry, geometry to trigonometry, and trigonometry to calculus. Calculus will make no sense without these other foundational subjects.

In this chapter we are going into the subject of figures of speech— legitimate grammatical constructions employed by an author for reasons of emphasis. Most people have been taught little, if anything, about figures of speech, yet one's unfamiliarity with something does not make it invalid. It is up to him to rise to the challenge of learning whatever the subject is, and then applying his knowledge for practical benefit.

Although this chapter may be a challenge for you, learning what it sets forth is integral to your understanding of God's goodness, and thus to your faith in and love for Him. We encourage you to proceed with aggressive anticipation.

If he is ever to truly understand the heart of God's Word, each reader of Scripture must understand that its pages are punctuated with figures of speech. In such figurative language, the words used do not mean what they would mean if they were taken literally. [66] For example, Isaiah 11:12 speaks of gathering people from "the the four corners of the earth." This statement obviously cannot be taken literally, yet its meaning is clear.

The reader is strongly encouraged to refer to E.W. Bullinger's seminal work *Figures Of Speech Used In The Bible* to begin to develop a sensitivity to the wide variety of figures God employs. Give particular attention to *Heterosis, Metonymy* and *Idiom,* for these figures show how much customary usages of words can be changed when employed by the Author of Holy Writ.

As we will see in this chapter, *Metonymy* and *Idiom* in particular hold the keys to understanding many of the difficult passages that seem to contradict God's loving nature. As stated earlier, the reader must be sensitive to the various literary devices that God uses in the text. There is not just one explanation that will then be true in every case. For example, God uses various forms of both *Metonymy* and *Idiom* regarding the subject with which we are dealing.

The figure of speech *Metonymy* involves the exchange of nouns or verbs, where one noun or verb is put for another related noun or

---

66. Although it is common to think of figures of speech as words that do not mean what they say, many figures of speech give emphasis in other ways. Figures such as Polysyndeton, Ellipsis and Polyptoton are good examples of this. The error to be guarded against is the common misconception that if something is figurative, any wild or fanciful explanation of the text is valid. This is not the case. The Bible is "God-breathed" (II Timothy 3:16), and God has the right to use figures of speech as He sees fit. It is the responsibility of the reader to learn to recognize these, as he must do with, say, geographical references throughout the Bible. It is up to the reader to take the time to learn about the geography so those references can be properly understood. The reader does not guess at geographical references and hope he is right. The same is true with figures of speech.

verb. The word "Metonymy" comes from *meta*, indicating change, and *onoma*, a name (or in grammar, a noun). *Metonymy* is a common figure of speech with a wide variety of usages. "The White House said today..." is one contemporary example in which the President of the United States and his staff are represented by the building they occupy. When we say, "Give me a hand," it is by the figure *Metonymy* that "hand" is put for the many useful ways the hand can help. [67]

As we will see, *Metonymy* is integrally involved in understanding many of the verses that seem to make God the direct and active cause of negative circumstances. *Metonymy* has many forms, and the biblical examples that concern us here are those related to the concepts of cause and effect, permission and prophecy. In the Old Testament, God often revealed Himself as the author of both good and evil. Thus "God" is often put by *Metonymy* as the cause of events that were actually engineered by the Devil.

To get a better understanding of the complexities of cause and effect, let us consider the case of Mr. Smith, who gets drunk at a party one night and then heads for home in his car, driving well above the posted speed limit on a two-lane highway. An oncoming car makes a left turn in front of him, but Mr. Smith's impaired perception causes him to misjudge the distance and swerve to avoid the other car. He loses control of his car, hits a concrete bridge abutment and is killed.

A policeman arriving at the scene might say that excessive alcohol was the cause of Mr. Smith's death. Mr. Smith's family might say the driver of the other car was the cause. The coroner's report would probably conclude that he died because he flew through the windshield and his head hit the concrete abutment.

In a sense, each of the statements is valid, although the coroner's report seems to most accurately reflect why Mr. Smith actually died. But did the concrete "kill" Mr. Smith? Not in the active sense in

---

67. One kind of Metonymy is the exchange of one noun for another related noun. For the most part, our use of this figure of speech is so natural that we do not even realize we are using it. We say "the whole school showed up for the senior prom" when we actually mean the *students*, not the "school" itself. *The American Heritage Dictionary of the English Language* [William Morris, ed., (American Heritage Pub. Co., Inc., Boston, 1969) page 826] gives the following example: "The words *sword* and *sex* are metonymical designations for military career and womankind in the example 'He abandoned the sword and the sex together.'" In his work *Figures of Speech Used in the Bible*, E.W. Bullinger gives four classes of metonymy: the cause, the effect, the subject, and the adjunct, and spends seventy pages on the subject.

which one person "kills" another. Yet the concrete *was* the final cause of his death, for if he had driven into a huge pile of mattresses instead of an immovable object, he might have survived. Nevertheless, we understand that the actual cause of his death was something other than the abutment, which did not jump into his path. The actual cause was whatever made him lose control of his car, which in his case was his heavily impaired faculties and judgment.

It has been said that one cannot "break" God's laws, but only breaks himself against them, because they are "immovable objects." God has set up the universe to function according to many laws and principles, which He said were "very good" (Genesis 1:31). In reality, physical laws cannot be broken. A farmer who disregards the principles of soil fertility will eventually go broke. The window cleaner with a cavalier attitude toward safety, whose worn-out rope breaks while he is dangling from the roof of a highrise office building, will, because of the law of gravity, be rudely introduced to an unsuspecting pedestrian.

There are spiritual laws also. For example: you reap what you sow; evil associations corrupt good ethics; sin separates man from God. When we "break" these laws, whether knowingly or unknowingly, we are not actually breaking *them*, rather we are breaking *ourselves* against them. Is God to blame because He set these laws in place? No more than a state highway department is liable for fatalities caused by drunken motorists driving into concrete bridge supports.

In the Bible, most especially in the Old Testament in regard to the cause of evil, sin and suffering, we find numerous records where the subject of a sentence is said to be the cause of an event, when in reality something else (another subject) is the cause. This is the figure of speech *Metonymy of the Subject*, in which one subject is put in place of another subject with which it stands in a definite relation.

A good illustration of how one subject is put for another is found in comparing the two seemingly contradictory biblical accounts of the death of King Saul. Remember that in the Old Testament, as we have noted, God was perceived as the ultimate cause of both positive and negative circumstances, and as sovereign in the sense that He controlled everything that happened. In I Samuel 31:4 and 5, the Word of God states that Saul died by committing suicide, falling upon his sword. Yet, I Chronicles 10:14 says that "the Lord put him to death" for disobeying the Word of God and for enquiring of a familiar spirit.

How do we reconcile these apparently conflicting statements? We do so by recognizing that the latter statement is the figure of speech *Metonymy of the Subject*. The actual subject, Saul (as stated in I Samuel 31) is exchanged for another subject, the Lord, with which it stands in a definite relation. The relation between Saul and the Lord is that it was the Lord God who gave Saul His commandments, and Saul disobeyed them. Thus the Lord can, in one sense, be said to be the "cause" of Saul's death. By breaking God's laws, Saul broke himself against them.

By his own choice, Saul separated himself from God and His blessings, and therefore faced the consequences of his actions without the benefit of God's grace and mercy. Because of his own sin, Saul found himself in a hopeless predicament, and killed himself. Only in the sense that God's Word was the "immovable object," against which Saul rebelled, could it be said that God "put him to death." In concluding this chapter, we will see *why* God used this figurative language in the Old Testament.

Just as there is a relation between Saul and God such that "Saul" can be exchanged for "God" by *Metonymy of the Subject*, so there is a relation between Satan and God such that they can be exchanged by *Metonymy of the Subject*. This relation between Satan and God, and why "Satan" is exchanged for "God" is explained later in this chapter.

For the most part, God's ability to alleviate for people the effects of sin is directly proportional to their obedience to Him. For instance, Romans 1:24 and 26 say that God "gave up" those who turned away from Him in the same way Jesus gave up His life, as an act of will (John 19:20). There are situations in which God reaches a point at which He knows it is fruitless to continue to attempt to convince people who are no longer willing to change their behavior. God lets them go on the road to self-destruction, to learn by experience apart from His grace and mercy, much like the father did in Jesus' parable about the prodigal son (Luke 15:11-32).

Why are people "permitted" to turn away? Because God highly values man's freedom of will. If one wills to continue in his sinful disobedience, he will suffer the consequences of his unwillingness to listen to God. God is not in the business of forcing obedience, which

then becomes meaninglessly mechanical. He does, however, honestly declare the consequences that result from sin so that all people
have a genuine choice. Without choice, there can be no true freedom.
God's desire is that His people be set free by knowledge, understanding and wisdom so they can make informed choices. He is fundamentally an educator, not an autocratic puppeteer.

Permission Or Prophetic Declaration?

An idiom is "a phrase or expression whose meaning cannot be
understood from the ordinary meanings of the words in it." [68] In
other words, the phrase does not mean what it appears to mean.
Every language has hundreds of idioms. At this point it is relevant
to take note of an idiom in the Hebrew language, in which "active
verbs were used...to express not the doing of the thing, but the
permission of the thing which the agent is said to do." [69]

---

68. *The World Book Dictionary*, Clarence L. Barnhart, Editor-in-chief (Doubleday and
Co. Inc., Chicago IL, 1970), page 1037.

69. Bullinger, *Figures Of Speech Used In The Bible*, page 823.

The active verb used in a permissive sense is widely attested to by scholars. In
The Emphasized Bible, a translation done by the eminent Hebrew scholar Joseph B.
Rotherham, the phrase "I will harden his [Pharaoh's] heart" is translated as "I will
let his heart wax bold" (Exodus 4:21). In defense of his translation, he offers the
following in a footnote: "...the translation in the text above would seem fairer to the
average Occidental mind, and is thoroughly justifiable on two grounds: (1) of the
known character of God, and (2) the well-attested latitude of the Semitic tongues,
which are accustomed to speak of *occasion* as *cause*" (p. 87). Rotherham goes on in
an appendix to say "...even *positive commands* are occasionally to be accepted as
meaning no more than *permission*" and he goes on to cite *Gesenius' Hebrew Grammar*
as more support for his translation.

Another source for studying the latitude of the active verb in the Hebrew
language is the "Hints and Helps to Bible Interpretation" section in the front of the
twenty-second American edition of *Young's Analytical Concordance to the Bible*,
(William B. Eerdmans Pub. Co., Grand Rapids MI, reprinted in 1975). Help number
70 gives eight uses of the active verb in Hebrew, with Scripture verses as examples
for further study. The eight uses show that the active verb expresses: a) only an
attempt to do the action, b) a permission, c) an announcement, d) giving an occasion,
e) a direction or sanction, f) a promise to do, g) a continuation, and h) what is done
by a deputy. Although we are primarily interested in the use of the active verb in
a permissive sense, it is important for the student of the Bible to be aware that some
languages use words in ways that other languages do not, and misunderstanding
how a language uses words can lead to misinterpretation and then to wrong
application.

In *Figures Of Speech Used In The Bible,* E.W. Bullinger assigns the permissive Hebrew idiom as the explanation of more than a few Scripture verses in which evil is attributed to God. For example, note the following verse, with Bullinger's comment:

Ezekiel 20:25

"Wherefore I gave them also statutes that were not good": *i.e.,* I permitted them to follow the wicked statutes of the surrounding nations, mentioned and forbidden in Lev. xviii.3.

God often warned Israel not to follow the pagan practices of other nations, but too often they chose, by the freedom of their will, to disobey Him. In such cases, one could say that God "permitted" them to suffer the consequences of their disobedience, just as He allows us to do. In the above verse, an active verb ("gave") is used idiomatically. God "permitted" Israel to do that which they were already determined to do.

Bullinger also assigns the permissive idiom as the explanation of a number of such verses. Some of these verses follow:

Exodus 5:22

"Lord, wherefore hast thou so evil entreated this people?" *i.e.,* suffered them to be so evil entreated.

Jeremiah 4:10

"Then said I, Ah, Lord God, surely thou hast greatly deceived this people": *i.e.,* thou hast suffered this People to be greatly deceived, by the false prophets, saying: Ye shall have peace, etc.

Ezekiel 14:9

"If the prophet be deceived when he hath spoken a thing, I the Lord have deceived that prophet": *i.e.,* I have permitted him to deceive himself.

2 Thessalonians 2:11 [70]

"For this cause God shall send them strong delusion, that they should believe a lie": *i.e.,* God will leave them and suffer them to be deceived by the great Lie which will come on all the world.

---

70. Regarding New Testament examples, E.W. Bullinger explains (*Figures of Speech Used in the Bible,* pages 819, 820) the use of this Hebraism: "The fact must ever be

While we recognize the figurative language in the above verses, we differ from Bullinger in our understanding of it, especially in regard to the idea of "permission."

Although the idea of "permission" may be preferable to thinking of God as the actual cause of evil, it is really a misleading concept, for two reasons. First, it implies that God is passively allowing something bad that He could stop, but chooses not to do so. Second, it also implies that God is not actively working to bring to pass good for His people.

To elaborate upon our differences with Bullinger, let us look at Jeremiah 4:10, which he cites in the above list as an example of the permissive idiom. The fact that he elsewhere cites it as an example of *Metonymy of the Subject* seems to indicate that he felt there is room for latitude in its explanation.

Jeremiah 4:10

Then said I, Ah, Lord God, surely thou hast greatly deceived this people, saying, Ye shall have peace; whereas the sword reacheth unto the soul.

Then Bullinger wrote:

The people deceived themselves, assuring themselves that they should have peace (5:12,31). The Lord had declared by his prophet that they would so deceive themselves, and so it came to pass that they were *permitted* to be deceived by their false prophets. [71]

---

remembered that, while the language of the New Testament is Greek, the agents and instruments employed by the Holy Spirit were Hebrews. God spake "by the mouth of his holy prophets." Hence, while the 'mouth' and the throat and vocal chords and breath were human, the *words* were Divine. No one is able to understand the phenomenon; or explain how it comes to pass: for Inspiration is a fact to be believed and received, and not a matter to be reasoned about. While therefore, the *words* are Greek, the *thoughts* and *idioms* are Hebrew. Some, on this account, have condemned the Greek of the New Testament, because it is not classical; while others, in their anxiety to defend it, have endeavored to find parallel usages in classical Greek authors. Both might have spared their pains by recognizing that the New Testament Greek abounds with Hebraisms: i.e., expressions conveying Hebrew usages and thoughts in Greek words. It will be seen at once that this is a subject which has a large and important bearing on the interpretation and clear understanding of many passages in the New Testament."

71. Bullinger, *Figures Of Speech Used In The Bible*, page 571.

Our understanding of this verse is that God's "permission" is specifically in the context of His prophetic activity. He did not just sit by and permit His people to be deceived, but rather He warned them in advance through Jeremiah (and other prophets as well). God "deceived" them only in the sense that they refused to listen to His true prophet who foretold of hard times and war, and chose instead to listen to the false prophets who foretold good things for them. [72] God did not literally deceive them by sending false prophets to lie to them, for this contradicts Numbers 23:19, which says "God is not a man that He should lie." [73]

The fatherly, loving nature of God is manifest in His faithfulness to prophetically declare to His people whatever they need to know in a given situation, such as the one cited above. One form of *Metonymy* is when an action itself is used instead of a prophecy or declaration that the action would occur. [74] Bullinger lists this as one of the forms of Metonymy of the Subject, specifically concerning verbs. We agree that it is in this category, but due to the very specific nature of this figure, and for the sake of clarity, we feel justified in identifying this as *Prophetic Metonymy*.

---

72. This also holds true for II Thessalonians 2:11: "God shall send them strong delusion, that they should believe a lie." God will permit them to believe the son of perdition after they have rejected Him.

73. We are fully aware that the people believed that God did send evil spirits and cause prophets to lie, as some Old Testament records like I Kings 22:19-23 indicate. This is our very point—that the Old Testament must be read in light of the New Testament to be correctly understood. The reader of Scripture must be aware that when the Bible quotes people, what they say reflects their perspective and belief, whether accurate or inaccurate. One of the "miserable comforters" said of Job, "You even undermine piety and hinder devotion to God" (Job 15:4). This statement, though in the Bible, is not correct, since Job did not "undermine piety." It represents the belief of the speaker. So there are times in the Old Testament where a person attributes evil to God based on his own understanding. In I Kings 22:23, the prophet Micaiah said, "The Lord has put a lying spirit in the mouth of all these prophets." Micaiah spoke according to the way God had revealed Himself to him. Likewise, King Saul's attendants said to him, "An evil spirit from God is tormenting you" (I Samuel 16:15). When the Word of God records people attributing evil to God, it is not an example of God using *Metonymy of the Subject*. Rather, it is simply what the people believed and said. We ask the reader to have patience and keep reading to see our explanation as to why the people believed the way they did concerning God and His relation to evil.

74. Bullinger, *Figures Of Speech Used In The Bible*, page 570.

For example, in Genesis 40 Joseph interpreted the prophetic dreams of Pharaoh's butler and baker, declaring that the former would be restored by Pharaoh and the latter would be hanged. When the butler was recounting Joseph's interpretation to Pharaoh, he said:

Genesis 41:13 (KJV)

And it came to pass, as he interpreted to us, so it was; me he restored unto mine office, and him he hanged.

It is not literally true that Joseph himself restored the butler and hung the baker, because it was Pharaoh who did so. But by the figure of speech *Metonymy*, the actions of hanging and restoring are said to be done by Joseph, because it was he who had prophetically declared that they would happen. [75]

Here is another example:

Isaiah 6:10

Make the heart of this people calloused; make their ears dull and close their eyes. Otherwise they might see with their eyes, hear with their ears, understand with their hearts, and turn and be healed.

This meant that Isaiah was to foretell that the heart of the children of Israel would become calloused, etc., not that he himself was to do this.

The following verse is a very clear example of Scripture attributing to God an action that, in reality, He had only prophetically declared:

Hosea 6:5

Therefore I cut you in pieces with my prophets, I killed you with the words of my mouth; my judgments flashed like lightning upon you.

Here we again see God warning His people and declaring to them the consequences that their disobedience to Him would bring

---

75. The *King James Version* renders the Hebrew text of Genesis 41:13 literally, using the translations "me he restored" and "him he hanged." Other translations see the difficulty caused by a literal rendering of the text and thus incorporate their understanding of the figure into the translation. For example, the N.I.V. reads: "I was restored" and "the other man was hanged."

upon them. God did not literally cut Israel in pieces— it was the Assyrians who came and did so, because Israel's sin and idolatry made them very vulnerable to Satan's assaults. Therefore, "I cut you in pieces" is an example of *Prophetic Metonymy*, and what God actually means is, "I foretold (and thus warned you) that you would be cut in pieces."

Another example of *Prophetic Metonymy* is Genesis 3:16: "I will greatly multiply thy sorrow...." The context of this statement clearly shows that God is prophesying or foretelling the consequences of man's sin, not declaring His will for all people's lives. We cannot fathom a loving God literally and deliberately inflicting a multiplying of sorrow on His children for generations because their ancestors disobeyed Him. We must search deeper in the context and refer to the scope of the Bible for the keys to the proper interpretation of this verse. In the context, we see that "I will greatly multiply thy sorrow" is a prophetic declaration meaning "your sorrow will be multiplied as a consequence of your sin." Much confusion is eliminated by understanding the use of *Prophetic Metonymy*.

"I Guess Perhaps You Should Let My People Go, Maybe"

Exodus 4:21, cited by Bullinger as an idiom of permission, is a verse we see as another great example of *Prophetic Metonymy*. Exodus 4:21 says that God "hardened Pharaoh's heart" so that Pharaoh would not let the people of Israel leave Egypt. Why would God do that when it was His idea in the first place that they leave?! [76] "I will harden Pharaoh's heart" should be understood to mean "I declare or

---

76. To this question, some would answer that God needed Pharaoh to resist so that He could demonstrate His great power. People who say this often quote the following verse: "But I have raised you up for this very purpose, that I might show you my power and that my name might be proclaimed in all the earth" (Exodus 9:16). We believe this verse is a genuine example of the permissive idiom. "I have raised thee up" means "I have permitted your rise to power." Since God did not foretell Pharaoh's rise to power, this is not an example of *Prophetic Metonymy*. In His great resourcefulness, God used the course of human events, in this case Egyptian history, to accomplish His purposes, among which were to provide an example of His power to deliver and of His righteous and holy nature (I Corinthians 10:11).

prophesy that Pharaoh will harden his heart in response to my attempt to free my people." [77]

In Exodus 3:11, God had declared prophetically to Moses before he ever set foot back in Egypt that Pharaoh's heart would be hardened and that he would not let Israel, God's "firstborn son" (Exodus 4:22), go free. God knew Pharaoh's heart and the pride thereof that would cause him to stubbornly resist, even to the extent of the death of his own firstborn son.

Though God knew this about Pharaoh, Pharaoh still had freedom of will. God therefore did His best to change Pharaoh's mind. He righteously and systematically gave Pharaoh plenty of chances and clear demonstrations of His power long before any Egyptians suffered any permanent harm. Several times in the record, Pharaoh appears to have repented.

We believe it is most relevant here to point out that God did not passively sit by while Pharaoh "hardened" his heart. On the contrary, God continued to aggressively act on behalf of His people, through whom the Christ would be born. It was like someone standing in front of someone else and pushing him in the chest with the palms of his hands until the other person decides either to get out of the way or fight. Pharaoh chose to fight, at least until the last plague. His corresponding hardening of heart increased sequentially in defiance to God (Exodus 8:15,32).

The plagues were designed to show the impotence of the Egyptian idols, the supremacy of God's power and the futility of resisting His declared will. The plagues also showed His mercy, being tailored to disrupt and humiliate the worship of their pagan deities without causing loss of human life until the final plague, which occurred only after God had exhausted every other option. When God moves, something has to give. People must decide either to believe and obey Him or to resist Him. There is no middle ground.

E.W. Bullinger's note on Exodus 4:21 is relevant: "It was in each case God's clemency and forbearing goodness which produced the

---

77. The record of the hardening of Pharaoh's heart is a good example of why the reader must be very sensitive to the text and the literary devices God is using in His Word. When God says to Moses "I will harden Pharaoh's heart," it is God using *Prophetic Metonymy*, speaking of what He knew would happen in the future. On the other hand, when Exodus 9:12 reads "The LORD hardened the heart of Pharaoh," it is *Metonymy of the Subject* where Satan and/or Pharaoh is actually hardening his heart.

hardening. That goodness which 'leadeth to repentance' (Romans 2:4): just as the same sun which softens the wax hardens the clay." [78] Those who do not recognize a figure of speech in the usage of the phrase "I will harden Pharaoh's heart" are forced into the unenviable position of explaining how a loving and righteous God can be guilty of causing a man to sin and then punishing him for it in order to accomplish His purposes.

To say that God forces a man (in this case Pharaoh) to repeatedly sin just so that He can "demonstrate" His power by striking the man down is to remove from God any concept of justice that can be grasped by the human mind. In his book *When Bad Things Happen To Good People*, Harold Kushner deals with this denial of the actual meaning of words. When his own son was suffering and dying, he looked for answers, and noted "...the books I turned to were more concerned with defending God's honor, with logical proof that bad is really good..." [79]

As we have stated, the New Testament reveals that Adam gave to Satan the power and authority over this world (Luke 4:6). Satan is called the "god of this age" (II Corinthians 4:4) because of the tremendous power he now wields. That means that people who do not look to the One True God, believe His Word and live accordingly are, in general, vulnerable to the attacks of the Devil. When someone rejects or disobeys God, he is like a soldier who, during a battle, leaves his fortress and walks into the camp of the enemy. He is placing himself in unnecessary danger. The prophet Jonah said that people who choose idols instead of God "forfeit the grace that could be theirs" (Jonah 2:8). Thus we understand that Pharaoh, by his free will, chose to oppose God's will and heeded the influence of God's enemy, the Devil.

Why God Used Metonymy Of The Subject

Remember that *Metonymy of the Subject* is when one subject is exchanged for another with which it stands in a definite relation.

---

78. E.W. Bullinger, *The Companion Bible* (Samuel Bagster and Sons Ltd., London, England, Reprinted 1964), page 77.

79. Kushner, *When Bad Things Happen To Good People*, page 4.

God does stand in a definite relation to Satan, but God could not reveal this relation to people in the Old Testament.

The relation between God and Satan should be clear from what we have set forth thus far in this book. God created Satan as a magnificent angel, Satan rebelled against God, and has ever since been diametrically opposed to all God is doing. The adversarial relationship between God and the Devil, and the battle they are waging, is the underlying reason for much of what we see in the course of human history.

In contrast to Old Testament language, the New Testament plainly identifies the Devil as the one plotting against God's people (II Corinthians 2:11; Ephesians 6:11). It shows the Devil to be the cause of death (Hebrews 2:14), sickness and oppression (Acts 10:38), spiritual blindness (II Corinthians 4:4) and opposition to the truth (John 8:44,45). Scripture makes plain that the Devil received his authority over the world from Adam, and that God, who can only act legally and righteously, cannot simply step in and take it away. Since the Devil has the authority over the earth, he does not need to ask God's permission to steal, kill and destroy. From his track record, even if he did have to ask, and was denied permission, *he would try to do evil anyway*!

Why would God not plainly reveal to His people in the Old Testament the truth about the Devil? The primary reason is that Jesus Christ had not yet come. It was Jesus who made known God as a loving Father (John 1:18), revealed the snare of the Devil (John 10:10a), exposed his devices (Luke 8:27-38) and, as the exalted Lord, made available to all men, from the day of Pentecost onward, the gift of holy spirit, (Acts 2:33). It is the supernatural power of the holy spirit, given to each person when he is "born again" (by adherence to Romans 10:9), that equips and enables the Christian not only to see with spiritual eyes the spiritual battle around him, but also to have power and authority over Satan and his evil spirit kingdom (Ephesians 6:10-17). Such was not the case before Jesus lived. God did not reveal to Old Testament believers their spiritual adversary and his hierarchy of henchmen. A record in Luke helps make this very clear.

Luke 10:1, 17-21, 23, 24:

After this the Lord appointed seventy-two others and sent them two by two ahead of him to every town and place where he was about to go.

The seventy-two returned with joy and said, "Lord, even the demons submit to us in your name."

He replied, "I saw Satan fall like lightning from heaven.

I have given you authority to trample on snakes and scorpions and to overcome all the power of the enemy; nothing will harm you.

However, do not rejoice that the spirits submit to you, but rejoice that your names are written in heaven."

At that time Jesus, full of joy through the Holy Spirit, said, "I praise you, Father, Lord of heaven and earth, because you have hidden these things from the wise and learned, and revealed them to little children. Yes, Father, for this was your good pleasure."

Then he turned to his disciples and said privately, "Blessed are the eyes that see what you see.

For I tell you that many prophets and kings wanted to see what you see but did not see it, and to hear what you hear but did not hear it."

Jesus sent out some of his disciples, and when they came back, they joyfully proclaimed that "even the demons submit to us in your name." That statement should catch the attention of every reader. No one in Scripture had ever said anything like that before— not Abraham, not Moses, not David, not Elijah, not any of the Old Testament "greats." Why not? Because they had not been given the necessary knowledge and authority that Jesus gave to His disciples.

As we saw in the above verses, Jesus told his disciples, "I have given you authority to trample on snakes and scorpions" (this refers to evil spirits - see verse 20). He also told them how blessed they were to know what they knew, since "many prophets and kings wanted to see what you see but did not see it" (verse 24). How true! The Old Testament rings with the anguished cries of those who did not understand the truth yet to be revealed about God and His relation to evil. "God has wronged me," cried Job (19:6). Elijah cried out, "...God, have you brought tragedy also upon this widow I am staying with, by causing her son to die?" (I Kings 17:20). "And Joshua said, 'Ah, Sovereign Lord, why did you ever bring this people across the Jordan to deliver us into the hands of the Amorites to destroy us?" (Joshua 7:7).

Today we can look back into the Old Testament, see *Metonymy of the Subject* and understand why God had to use this figure of speech. It seems clear that without the power to fight the Devil, people were better off not knowing about him. In His abounding love, God "took the rap" for good and evil, telling His people that if they believed and obeyed Him, they would be blessed, but if they disobeyed Him, He would afflict them. God's use of *Metonymy of the Subject* emphasized His efforts to communicate to His people both the consequences of their sin and the fact that, if they disobeyed Him, He would have to give them up to their disobedience and let them learn the hard way. In the Old Testament, "windows" allowing us to see the spiritual battle going on "behind the scenes" are few, but they do exist. For example, there is the record in Daniel 10:1-14 (see Chapter Eleven).

Another window that gives us a view of the actual spiritual conflict in the Old Testament is found in the record of King David taking a census of the fighting men of Israel and Judah. II Samuel 24:1 reads, "Again the anger of the LORD burned against Israel, and he incited David against them, saying, "Go and take a census of Israel and Judah." This seems to blatantly contradict I Chronicles 21:1 which says "Satan rose up against Israel and incited David..." For one thing, if the Lord really did incite David to sin, then how, in any sense, can God be said to be holy and loving? The consequence of this particular sin of David's was the death of seventy thousand people!

God says over and over that He wants people to stop sinning. He also says He loves people and wants people to live, not die. Unless God is just a blatant liar, there has to be another explanation for "the Lord incited David [to sin]..." Thankfully, the other explanation is given in the Chronicles record, which fingers Satan as the real culprit. "The Lord" is used in the Samuel record by *Metonymy of the Subject*. This serves as a reminder to us that the laws and principles that God has set up are immutable and immobile and that if we "break" them, we will end up being broken against them.

The Old Testament saints did not recognize that God was using such figures of speech as *Metonymy of the Subject* to conceal the truth about Satan. God's people actually thought that God was the cause of both good and evil. It is very important to understand this point, because the people speaking and writing a language are usually aware of its figures of speech. However, when it comes to figures of speech God used in His Word, such as *Metonymy of the Subject*, people would have had no way to understand them unless God Himself had explained them. We have seen why He did not do so until He made things clear through the teachings of Jesus Christ and the New Testament. Remember that "truth" came through Jesus Christ (John 1:17).

What we have set forth in this chapter shows how grievous error can occur when a person is ignorant of the figurative language God utilized in regard to the problem of evil, sin and suffering. God becomes a tyrannical being who hardens hearts, sends evil spirits, deceives people, gives wicked laws, leads people into temptation, etc. Sadly, some people still think God actually does those terrible things. If He does, the Bible overflows with contradictions in heart and logic. In closing this chapter, we want to emphasize the following principle: *Whenever God is said to do something at cross-purposes with His stated character or goals,* a figure of speech is involved, which is a legitimate grammatical construction, and can be understood within the scope of Scripture.

CHAPTER **6**

WHAT ABOUT JOB?

Must Satan Ask God's Permission To Do Evil?

A very well known biblical record that needs to be considered at this point is the Book of Job. [80] In Chapters One and Two, "Satan" is referred to as one of the angels who presented himself before the Lord. In light of the New Testament, we today realize that "Satan" is one of the names Scripture gives to the Devil, but the Hebrew word for "Satan" (as in the Book of Job) simply means "accuser." Those in the Old Testament thought that "Satan" was only an accusing spirit. They had no concept of him as the mighty spiritual enemy he is.

Misunderstanding, as literal rather than figurative, the "conversations" between God and Satan in the book of Job has caused many people no end of confusion, because it certainly sounds as if the

---

80. *The Book of Job: Why Me?* (CES Bi-Monthly Tape, Jul/Aug 1991).

Devil must ask permission from God to do evil, and furthermore, that God sometimes *grants* him such permission. The New Testament, however, reveals Satan as the "god of this age," who does not ask God's permission before doing evil. If he did, the so-called "war" raging between the forces of good and evil would be a sham.

This is why the dialogue between God and Satan must be an allegory, set forth in Scripture as it is because of the limited understanding of the Old Testament believers. [81] The way most people have interpreted the Book of Job leaves God looking like a bored puppeteer who gets his kicks by tormenting one of his puppets and killing a lot of innocent bystanders just to win a bet with the Devil. [82] By the way, if the Devil did have to get God's permission in order to do evil, evil would be easy to stop. God could "Just say No!"

The allegory in the opening two chapters of the book of Job serves to illustrate Job's unconditional love for God. The Book of Job was written to show that Job did not love God only because of what God had done for him. Rather, Job loved God because He is God, and thus is worthy of love no matter what the circumstances were in Job's life.

The fact that Job did not understand the truth revealed in the New Testament about "Satan" is why he would say, regarding the loss of his wealth and the death of his sons and daughters, "...the Lord gave, and the Lord has taken away; may the name of the Lord be praised" (Job 1:21). It is also why the next verse says that "In all this Job did not sin by charging God with wrongdoing." Not knowing about the Devil's kingdom and devices, Job could only attribute all his hardship to God.

The Devil has a vested interest in keeping everyone as ignorant about his *modus operandi* as he possibly can. One way he does this is by afflicting both good people and bad people in such a manner that

---

81. An allegory can be difficult to spot in Scripture. Galatians 4:24 states that Abraham's two sons "are an allegory" (KJV). Thus what seems to be literal and on the surface in the Old Testament, God reveals in the New Testament as something that actually involves a deeper truth. So it is with Job. God could not reveal the true nature and power of the Devil, but He could reveal some things about him. We refer you to Bullinger's *Figures of Speech Used in the Bible* (pages 748-750) for an excellent explanation of an allegory.

82. Yancey, *Disappointment With God*, pages 187, 188.

it is impossible to determine whether a person is good or evil simply by what is happening in his life. It is very important to understand this point, if we as Christians are going to be true sources of help and blessings to others who are in need. Suffering, in and of itself, is not a valid barometer of one's sinfulness nor his godliness, nor is it an indicator of God's judgment on one's life (Luke 13:1-5). Often Satan will arrange the circumstances so that a person doing evil suffers no apparent consequences (Psalm 37:7; Job 21). In other cases, he sees to it that one doing the right thing suffers for it (II Corinthians 11:23-28).

Miserable "Comforters"

Job was "blameless," yet he suffered horribly. Job's "friends," not realizing that personal suffering is not an automatic indicator of personal sin or of God's judgment, accused him of sin. [83] Regarding the attitude and approach of Job's friends, Rabbi Kushner writes:

> They start out truly wanting to comfort Job and make him feel better. They try to reassure him by quoting all the maxims of faith and confidence on which they and Job alike were raised. They want to comfort Job by telling him that the world does in fact make sense, that it is not a chaotic, meaningless place. What they do not realize is that they can only make sense of the world, and of Job's suffering, by deciding that he deserves what he has gone through. To say that everything works out in God's world may be comforting to the casual bystander, but it is an insult to the bereaved and the unfortunate. "Cheer up, Job, nobody ever gets anything he doesn't have coming to him" is not a very cheering message to someone in Job's circumstances.

> But it is hard for the friends to say anything else. They believe, and want to continue believing, in God's goodness and power. But if Job is innocent, then God must be guilty—

---

83. Obviously, one's personal sin can lead to suffering. For example, sexual sin can lead to sexually transmitted diseases and terrible suffering, but that is not the point here. Personal suffering is not *necessarily* an indicator of personal sin, as the records of Job, Jesus Christ and others clearly show.

guilty of making an innocent man suffer. With that at stake, they find it easier to stop believing in *Job's* goodness than to stop believing in God's perfection. [84]

Blaming the victim is a way of reassuring ourselves that the world is not as bad a place as it may seem, and that there are good reasons for people's suffering. It helps fortunate people believe that their good fortune is deserved, rather than being a matter of luck. It makes everyone feel better— except the victim, who now suffers the double abuse of social condemnation on top of his original misfortune. This is the approach of Job's friends, and while it may solve their problem, it does not solve Job's, or ours. [85]

The reaction of Job's "friends" is *still* often the reaction of the friends and relatives of someone who is suffering. Believing that God sends suffering to punish those who sin, they often "blame" the person who is suffering. Eliphaz said, "Who, being innocent, has ever perished?" (Job 4:7). Bildad argued, "Does God pervert justice?" and "Surely God does not reject a blameless man" (Job 8:4,20). (Of course we know from Job 1:1 that Job was "blameless.") Then Zophar chimed in: "If you put away the sin that is in your hand...you will stand firm" (Job 11:14,15).

Job correctly reasons that it is easy for those who are well off to criticize others who are suffering. In response to such criticism, Job said, "I also could speak like you, if you were in my place; I could make fine speeches against you" (Job 16:4). More important at this point, though, is what God says in Job 42:7.

Job 42:7

After the Lord had said these things to Job, he said to Eliphaz the Temanite, "I am angry with you and your two friends, because you have not spoken of me what is right, as my servant Job has.

God very plainly says that Job's friends wrongly blamed Job when he was suffering. Of course, there are times when people are obviously suffering for a sin they have committed, but God's answer

---

84. Kushner, *When Bad Things Happen To Good People*, page 38.

85. *Ibid.*, pages 39,40.

to Job's "comforters" should be a stern warning to those who have concluded that people always get what they deserve in this life.

Job knew he was blameless, and yet he was suffering. He said "...God has wronged me...," (Job 19:6) [86] and he called his friends "miserable comforters" (Job 16:2). Job tried to teach his friends that suffering is not always the result of personal sin, and his speech, recorded in Job 21, should have shut up Eliphaz, Bildad and Zophar, as well as the thousands of other sincere but misguided "comforters" since that time. Here are some excerpts:

Job 21 (condensed)

Then Job replied: "Listen carefully to my words...why do the wicked live on, growing old and increasing in power? Their homes are free from fear...their bulls never fail to breed, their cows calve and do not miscarry. They send forth their children as a flock; their little ones dance about. They spend their years in prosperity and go down to the grave in peace. Yet they say to God, 'leave us alone! We have no desire to know your ways. Who is the Almighty, that we should serve him?' One man dies in full vigor, completely secure and at ease...Another man dies in bitterness of soul, never having enjoyed anything good. So how can you console me with your nonsense. Nothing is left of your answers but falsehood!"

Job was not the only Old Testament person to know that people do not always get what they deserve. For example, the following verse in Ecclesiastes, written by Solomon, is very clear:

Ecclesiastes 8:14

There is something else meaningless that occurs on earth: righteous men who get what the wicked deserve, and wicked men who get what the righteous deserve. This too, I say, is meaningless.

---

86. It is interesting to note that Job knew he had been wronged, even though he thought that God was the one who had wronged him. How blessed he would have been to know the truth revealed in the New Testament! No wonder Christ said to his disciples, after revealing the truth about the Devil to them, "Blessed are the eyes that see what you see" (Luke 10:23).

Although Job knew that the calamity that had befallen him was not due to sin in his life, he did not understand why God (the only possible source of his suffering based on his understanding of life) had afflicted him. Throughout the Book of Job, he continues to ask God, "Why me?" and often does so very angrily.

Is Everything That Happens God's Will?

Does God answer Job's questions? Not in Job's lifetime, nor throughout the Old Testament Scriptures. Jesus Christ, however, taught truths that do answer Job's questions. Kushner has some excellent insight on the record of Job:

> To try to understand the book and its answer, let us take note of three statements which everyone in the book, and most of the readers, would like to be able to believe:
>
> A. God is all-powerful and causes everything that happens in the world. Nothing happens without His willing it.
>
> B. God is just and fair, and stands for people getting what they deserve, so that the good prosper and the wicked are punished.
>
> C. Job is a good person.
>
> As long as Job is healthy and wealthy, we can believe all three of those statements at the same time with no difficulty. When Job suffers, when he loses his possessions, his family and his health, we have a problem. We can no longer make sense of all three propositions together. We can now affirm any two only by denying the third.
>
> If God is both just and powerful, then Job must be a sinner who deserves what is happening to him. If Job is good but God causes his suffering anyway, then God is not just. If Job deserved better and God did not send his suffering, then God is not all-powerful. We can see the argument of the Book of Job as an argument over which of the three statements we are prepared to sacrifice, so that we can keep on believing in the other two.

Job's friends are prepared to stop believing in (C), the assertion that Job is a good person. They want to believe in God as they have been taught to. They want to believe that God is good and that God is in control of things. And the only way they can do that is to convince themselves that Job deserves what is happening to him. [87]

Job, for his part, is unwilling to hold the world together theologically by admitting that he is a villain. He knows a lot of things intellectually, but he knows one thing more deeply. Job is absolutely sure that he is not a bad person. He may not be perfect, but he is not so much worse than others, by any intelligible moral standard, that he should deserve to lose his home, his children, his wealth and health while other people get to keep all those things. And he is not prepared to lie to save God's reputation.

Job's solution is to reject proposition (B), the affirmation of God's goodness. Job is in fact a good man, but God is so powerful that He is not limited by considerations of fairness and justice. [88]

Kushner correctly states that Job considered himself an innocent victim and that Job thought that God afflicts both the righteous and unrighteous. Often Job attested to his own innocence. He said, "I had not denied the words of the Holy One" (Job 6:10b); "Show me where I have been wrong" (Job 6:24); "I am blameless" (Job 9:21); "You [God] know that I am not guilty" (Job 10:7); "Can anyone bring charges against me? If so, I will be silent and die" (Job 13:19); "As surely as God lives, who has denied me justice" (Job 27:2); and "Let God weigh me in honest scales and He will know that I am blameless" (Job 31:6). Job made his case that God does whatever He pleases and afflicts both the innocent and the guilty: "...I say, He destroys both the blameless and the wicked" (Job 9:22).

Under this assumption, Job wished there were a mediator or an umpire that could help him out. "If only there were someone to arbitrate between us, to lay his hand upon us both" (Job 9:33). Of course, no umpire or mediator appears. What does appear is a storm, and God Himself speaking from it (Job 38:1). What did God say to Job

---

87. Kushner, *When Bad Things Happen To Good People*, pages 37,38.

88. *Ibid.*, page 40.

in answer to his pleading questions? Well, one thing is clear— God did not give Job any reason for the problems besetting him.

Many theologians and Bible teachers rightly point out that God never gave Job an answer to the question of why he was suffering: "...God never answers question one about Job's predicament..." [89] "With all due respect to the many capable and godly preachers and writers who have taught that the major question as addressed in Job is why do the righteous suffer, we note that if this *is* the question, it is never answered in the Book of Job." [90]

Why not? Because the truth about the Devil as the source of human suffering was not revealed in the Old Testament. It was Jesus Christ who first openly revealed the true source of mankind's suffering.

Interestingly enough, Rabbi Kushner comes to the same conclusion we do, that proposition (A) is the proposition that is in error— "God is all-powerful and causes everything that happens in the world. Nothing happens without His willing it." We do not, however, agree with his overall understanding of the book of Job, by which he arrives at this conclusion. We arrive at our conclusion from the teachings of Jesus and the New Testament. Nonetheless, we applaud Kushner's insight about people's reaction to this conclusion. He states:

> There may be a sense of loss at coming to this conclusion. In a way, it was comforting to believe in an all-wise, all-powerful God who guaranteed fair treatment and happy endings, who reassured us that everything happened for a reason, even as life was easier for us when we could believe that our parents were wise enough to know what to do and strong enough to make everything turn out right. But it was comforting the way the religion of Job's friends was comforting: it worked only as long as we did not take the problems of innocent victims seriously. When we have met Job, when we have *been* Job, we cannot believe in that sort of God any longer

89. Yancey, *Disappointment With God* (Harper Paperbacks, New York NY, 1988), page 223.

90. Henry M. Morris, *The Remarkable Record of Job* (Baker Book House, Grand Rapids MI, 1988), page 22.

without giving up our own right to feel angry, to feel that we have been treated badly by life. [91]

The New Testament makes it crystal clear that not everything that happens is God's will. For example, Jesus instructed his disciples to pray that God's will would be done on earth (Matthew 6:10). If everything that happens is God's will, such prayer is superfluous. In Romans 1:10, Paul said he prayed for "a prosperous journey in the will of God" to see the believers there. Another meaningless prayer? No. The will of God for an individual, whether revealed in the written Word of God or by direct revelation, generally comes to pass only when that person understands it and, by his own free will, acts accordingly.

Rather than sit passively by waiting for God's will to happen, we must make a diligent effort to learn God's Word and then aggressively obey it. God's will, for example, is that people do not steal, but rather that they work to earn what they need (Ephesians 4:28). Very simple. We just do what He says. But are some people stealing? Yes. If everything that happens were God's will, then *nothing* would be sin or disobedience. What a travesty of logic!

Going a step further then, if it is so easy for us humans to disobey God, what about the Devil and his spirit army? Can humans sin by choice while evil spirits cannot? Obviously spirit beings can sin, since sin was the reason the Devil and his hosts were thrown out of God's presence to begin with. Via Adam's sin, the Devil was legally given authority over the earth. The Devil did not and does not obey God. The Devil has been sinning for a long time (I John 3:8). The Devil is a murderer (John 8:44), a liar (John 8:44), and a thief (John 10:10).

God's Answer To Job's Question

Because of the teaching of Jesus Christ, Paul, and other New Testament writers, we today know about the spiritual battle raging around us. Job, however, did not know about the Devil. How did God answer Job? The "answer" that God gave Job was actually a series of questions God asks him. Franz Delitzsch writes:

---

91. Kushner, *When Bad Things Happen To Good People,* page 44.

When now Jehovah condescends to negotiate with Job by question and answer, He does not do exactly what Job wished (ch. 13:22), but something different, of which Job never thought. He surprises him with questions...questions among which there are many which the natural philosophy of the present day can frame more scientifically, but cannot satisfactorily solve. [92]

Job, of course, is at a loss to answer the questions God poses (and, in most cases, so are we today). He says to God: "I am unworthy—how can I reply to you?" (Job 40:4). Job is overawed by God's presence and power. He admits his limited knowledge and understanding. "Surely I spoke of things I did not understand, things too wonderful [better translated "extraordinary"] for me to know" (Job 42:3). Thus God, by His presence and power, "answered" Job by clearly demonstrating that He is God. The implication is, "Look, I'm God and you're not. You get about your business and I'll get about mine."

But somehow God's "answer" to Job is not satisfactory to us. We believe that God does, however, give us the answer as to why there is human suffering, but not in the Book of Job or anywhere else in the Old Testament. He gives it in the New Testament. What then is the point of the book of Job?

The main point of the book of Job is that *no matter what happened to Job, he refused to harden his heart and turn away from God.* It is absolutely imperative that each and every Christian realize this and learn from Job. Job lost everything— his wealth, his children, his health, the respect of his wife— but he never gave up on God. Yes, he held God responsible because that was all he knew, but he also felt that if he could ever get a "fair trial," he and God could straighten things out.

Job 23:3-7

If only I knew where to find Him; if only I could go to his dwelling!

I would state my case before Him and fill my mouth with arguments.

92. C.F. Keil and F. Delitzsch, *Commentary On The Old Testament,* Vol. IV, "Job," Book Two, (William B. Eerdmans, Grand Rapids MI, reprint 1975), page 312.

I would find out what he would answer me, and consider what he would say.

Would He oppose me with great power? No, He would not press charges against me.

There an upright man could present his case before him, and I would be delivered forever from my judge.

In times of suffering, many people stop looking to God. Despite thinking that his affliction came from God, Job's confidence that if he and God could meet together they could "work things out" is inspiring and instructional.

One of the lessons we can draw from the book of Job is that the Devil acts according to his own purposes and agenda, "seeking whom he may devour" (I Peter 5:8). The parable of the sower is one of many biblical sections that reveal that the primary object of Satan's attack is the Word of God (Luke 8:12). His first recorded utterance in the Scripture is a challenge to God's Word: "Yea, has God said?" (Genesis 3:2). His attacks can be directed at anyone, and are designed to create doubt in people as to the goodness and power of God. These attacks may be theological (e.g., miserable comforters) or circumstantial (e.g., boils, storms, etc.,), and may be through either pressures or pleasures.

In any case, each believer is to resist the attack of the Adversary and boldly declare God's Word. No one will grow in faith without a firm resolve to endure and move forward with the Lord despite resistance. As the saying goes, "Following the path of least resistance is what makes men and rivers crooked." Shrinking from adversity or persecution is often due to desiring the praise of men more than the praise of God (John 12:43; Galatians 6:12). Job is an example of one who maintained his integrity in the teeth of a vicious attack by the enemy, for which he bore no responsibility. God was faithful to restore to him double all his blessings, so that his latter end was greater than his beginning, despite Satan's attack. The last chapter of the Book of Job foreshadows the ultimate deliverance and victory promised to every believer via resurrection. [93] It also shows that in this life we have the right to expect God to deliver us from suffering.

---

93. Job 42:10 says that God gave Job twice as much of everything as he had before his affliction, yet verse 13 says that he had seven sons and three daughters, the same number who had died (1:2). This is no contradiction, because in the resurrection the number of his children will be doubled.

Why Me, Lord?

If the question of why there is evil, sin and suffering is answered only in the New Testament, does that mean that there is no value for the Christian in reading and studying the book of Job? Not at all. There is tremendous value for each and every Christian in the book of Job. Beside the clear teaching that suffering comes upon both good and evil people, and how not to be a miserable comforter, the fact that Job never blamed himself for his suffering is an extremely valuable lesson. Furthermore, Job's faithfulness in looking to God is a great example for us who, although we know that the Devil and sin are the root causes of suffering, still may wonder "Why me? Why now?" when something terrible happens in our lives.

Life abounds with situations where the direct cause of the suffering is unknown. "Why was *my* child crossing the street when the person ran the stop sign?" "Why am *I* the one with cancer?" "Why did the tornado hit *my* house and leave so many others untouched?" "I eat what all my friends eat, why did *I* have a heart attack?" As we stated, knowing that the root cause of suffering is the sin of the Devil and of Adam does not answer the immediate questions of "Why me?" and "Why now?" Realistically, precise answers to those questions may never be determined in this life. But what a relief to know that God is not causing your suffering. Instead of turning to God and angrily asking, "Why did you do this to me?" we can take God at His Word when He says He is a loving God and Father and gives good and perfect gifts. We can turn to Him in times of trouble and ask for help, knowing that He is both able and willing to give it.

Rabbi Kushner comments about this:

From that perspective, there ought to be a sense of relief in coming to the conclusion that God is not doing this to us. If God is a God of justice and not of power, then He can still be on our side when bad things happen to us. He can know that we are good and honest people who deserve better. Our misfortunes are none of His doing, and so we can turn to Him for help. Our question will not be Job's question, "God, why are You doing this to me?" but rather, "God, see what is happening to me. Can You help me?" We will turn to God, not to be judged or forgiven, not to be rewarded or punished, but to be strengthened and comforted...

We can maintain our own self-respect and sense of goodness without having to feel that God has judged us and condemned us. We can be angry at what has happened to us, without feeling that we are angry at God. More than that, we can recognize our anger at life's unfairness, our instinctive compassion at seeing people suffer, as coming from God who teaches us to be angry at injustice and to feel compassion for the afflicted. Instead of feeling that we are opposed to God, we can feel that our indignation is God's anger at unfairness working through us, that when we cry out, we are still on God's side, and He is still on ours. [94]

Job never knew that the Devil, not God, was the real cause of his problems. We today should learn from the New Testament that which Job was never taught— that there is a real war going on between good and evil, and that the Devil, not God, is the true source of evil. We who do understand that God is love should never blame Him for evil or turn away from Him in time of trouble. If, however, one does not grasp the vital truths set forth thus far in this book, he may do exactly that.

Our God is not only a God of justice, but also a God of power, awesome power, which He demonstrated in the resurrection, ascension and exaltation of Jesus Christ as Lord. Within the bounds of the laws He set up, and in conjunction with our free-will faith in Him, God and His Son are powerfully active in the lives of His people. Scripture is replete with examples.

Again we want to emphasize how imperative it is for the student of the Bible to distinguish between that which is literal and that which is figurative. Whenever something is attributed to God that is inconsistent with His nature, purposes or will as revealed in the whole of Scripture, it must be a figure of speech. Understanding this resolves the apparent contradiction between the Old Testament and the New Testament, reveals God's true heart of love for His people and removes for man a major obstacle to wholehearted love for his magnificent Creator.

---

94. Kushner, *When Bad Things Happen To Good People*, pages 42-45.

CHAPTER 7

THE JUSTICE AND JUDGMENTS OF GOD

Justice Demands Judgment

We have emphasized the point that God is righteous, and we have identified the role of law in God's dealings with His creation. His actions must conform to the strictest legal requirements of justice. God is called "the judge of all the earth" (Genesis 18:25), and justice demands that wrongdoers receive retribution. A primary definition of "judgment" is the determination of guilt or innocence according to a standard of moral law or principle. Each and every wrongdoer will receive just retribution when he one day stands before the throne of judgment.

Biblically, the "standard of moral law or principle" is Jesus Christ. He is the chief subject of Scripture from Genesis 3:15 to the end, and God's judgments are relative to His purposes in Christ. For example, we can see that throughout the Old Testament, God's "judgments" were relative to His protection of the bloodline from which the Messiah would come (e.g., at Babel, the Egyptians, Amalek, et al). This fits with His promise to Abraham to "curse them that cursed him [his descendants]" (Genesis 12:3). Other people mentioned in the Bible were evil, but there is no record that they received God's judgment unless they infringed upon His purposes for Israel (and thus for Christ). It was like, "You can do anything that ya wanna do, but uh-uh, honey, lay offa them Jews!" (Our apologies to Elvis).

Once Jesus was personally present during the gospels period, He said that He did not come to judge the world, but to save it (John 12:47). Jesus came to declare "the acceptable year of the Lord" (Luke 4:19), deferring the "day of vengeance of our God" (Isaiah 61:2) to a future day of judgment. This same truth is manifest in John 5:22: "the Father judgeth no man," and II Corinthians 5:19: "not imputing their trespasses unto them." Romans further reveals that the first time Christ came, it was not for condemnation, but for reconciliation, blessing and salvation to those who by faith judge themselves worthy of it.

Since the day of Pentecost when the new birth became available, those who believe in Jesus as Lord are freely justified and are judged by God to be *in Christ*. Thus, they have "the righteousness of God" (II Corinthians 5:21). By His perfect obedience, Christ met God's standard of righteousness. Although no other man by his own works can do likewise, each who believes in Christ as Lord has Christ's righteousness imputed to him. Thus one is not judged for salvation by how close his life and conduct conforms to Christ's, but whether he accepts Christ's work on his behalf, and the judicial grace made available in Him. Those who accept this grace are at once and forever judged to be innocent, they are identified with Christ in all that He is and they are made worthy in His worthiness. The only future judgment that remains for someone in Christ is whether his actions from the time of his new birth are worthy of everlasting rewards (I Corinthians 3:13), which he will enjoy in his everlasting life.

Future Judgment

God has, with few exceptions, reserved His judgment for the future. [95] Christ explained this in "the parable of the tares" (Matthew 13:31-43). The "tares" are the "sons of the evil one," and they are allowed to grow with the "sons of the kingdom" until the judgment. At that time, and not before, they will be judged by the Lord Jesus Christ, to whom God has delegated the responsibility of judging all men (John 5:22; Acts 10:42; II Timothy 4:8). As the One and only man to perfectly obey God, He has earned the right to judge all other men, including those who opposed Him and God. This truth that the Lord will judge all men on the appointed Day of Judgment is clearly portrayed in a number of verses in the Bible. For example:

Acts 17:31

For he has set a day when he will judge the world with justice by the man he has appointed. He has given proof of this to all men by raising him from the dead.

Although in "the administration of God's grace" (Ephesians 3:2, i.e., the Church Age that began on the day of Pentecost as recorded in Acts 2) we do not see God doing anything like the Flood, He will one day send His Son Jesus Christ to finally judge all men, and, as did the Flood, Christ will destroy all evil people. Throughout His Word, God makes it clear that each man will one day be held accountable for the way he has lived his life. Those who reject God's grace in Christ remain in the condemnation they inherited from Adam, and thus will face judgment in the future on the merit of their works alone. At that time, God's loving justice will prevail once and for all (II Thessalonians 1:6-10).

How God Judges Now

To say that God is not now judging, in the sense of condemning and punishing people, is not to say that He is not judging at all. God

---

95. There are several future judgments mentioned in the Bible. Each person ("Jew, Gentile and Church of God"— I Corinthians 10:32) will be a part of one of them depending upon when he lived and whether or not he believed God's revelation for that time.

has to make a variety of judgments, that is, decisions, relative to His activities in each age or time frame. A more general definition of "judgment" is discrimination or choice, and God must make choices. He must determine whether faith is present in someone's life for salvation and blessings (Romans 10:9,10; James 1:7; Romans 4:16). He must choose whom and when to call to what functions of service to Him (Jeremiah 1:5; I Corinthians 12:18, 28).

In one sense, God has allowed man to judge himself by his response to the Word of God. Paul says that the Jews had "judged themselves unworthy of eternal life" (Acts 13:46) by refusing to have faith in Jesus as their Messiah. In Christ, God has reached out to man with many infallible proofs of His Messiahship and resurrection (Acts 1:3). It is now man's "move" whether to accept or reject God's grace. God leaves it up to each person to judge for himself, based on the evidence He has provided. In contrast to all the religious leaders in history, only Jesus Christ has been raised from the dead with an immortal physical body verified by many eye-witnesses.

Another point to be made is that, because God is not actively judging sinners at this time, He has delegated a certain measure of judgment to civil government. It was God's idea that there be civil authority, primarily so that those who desire to love and serve Him could do so in "quiet and peaceable" surroundings (I Timothy 2:2— KJV). Although many people in government positions are corrupt, we can still see the benefits of civil authority in general.

God has given people the responsibility to run their own societies (Genesis 9:5,6; Romans 13:1ff, et al). It is up to man to make and enforce regulations and laws that promote peace and prosperity and deter criminal activity. Godly laws, if followed, would help to maintain justice, as well as be guidelines to show how society can function in a just manner. [96] If God were actively judging today, it is likely that criminal activity on all levels would be drastically reduced.

While they allow people to judge for themselves as to their own salvation (by their response to Christ), God and the Lord Jesus do make judgments for blessings now. The primary basis on which they do so is faith. Hebrews 4:16 indicates that there is a distinction between the *thoughts* and the *intents* of the heart. God can discern

---

96. *The Bible and Civil Law* (CES Bi-Monthly Tape, Mar/Apr 1990).

between genuine faith and unbelief, even when the latter is masked by religious practices (Matthew 23:23).

In looking upon the heart of each person, God holds people accountable for the knowledge and understanding of His Word that they have. Luke 12:48 says that to whom much is given much shall be required. God is a personal God who is concerned with personal relationships. He created man in order to have fellowship with him. He gave man free will, and ordered the universe in such a way that the physical world clearly points out His existence and beneficence (Acts 14:15-17; Romans 1:20). Furthermore, it is clear that God has put within man the ability to know the difference between good and evil, or God could not fairly ask him to choose between them.

Since man has inherent knowledge of basic right and wrong, and since the evidence of a Creator is all around us, God can expect humans to want to know Him, search for Him and then love, respect and obey Him. God wants to help people know and understand Him, because God genuinely wants fellowship with those He has created. We must recognize that obedience to God is not just adherence to general requirements (not stealing, etc.), but is also a personal matter in regard to our relationship with Him. Therefore, sin is more than disobeying an impersonal law; it is the destruction of a relationship.

We have to accept personal responsibility for our sins, and also recognize that what may be sin in one's life is not necessarily sin in someone else's (Romans 14:20-23). God's Word defines some actions that are always sin; for example: murder, adultery and drunkenness, while other behaviors may or may not be sin, depending on the heart of the person and the situation. In his book *Counter Attack: Taking Back Ground Lost To Sin,* Jay Carty has some wonderful insight on the concept of absolute and variable sin: Carty relates variable sin to behavior that takes control of you (contrast that to your responsibility to bring every thought captive to Christ—II Corinthians 10:5). He writes: "If something takes mastery in your life, my friend, it has just become sin." [97] Every person has different strengths and weaknesses. It is our responsibility to recognize what our weaknesses are and not allow ourselves to be enslaved by them.

---

[97]. Jay Carty, *Counter Attack: Taking Back Ground Lost To Sin* (Multnomah Press, Portland OR, 1988) page 102.

Grace, Reward, Mercy and Wrath

God is not a referee or an umpire, simply enforcing impersonal laws. He is a *Father*. As such, He knows the hearts of His children and deals with each one accordingly. Every good parent knows there are times when a child who is really trying to do what is right needs that extra bit of help. That extra help could be called *grace*. The parents may then *reward* the child for doing right. Also, there are times when a child, who really is a "good kid," does something wrong. Sometimes in such situations, a little *mercy* is called for, rather than the full weight of "the law" crashing down on him. Another child may be continually rebellious and hateful, despite his parents' attempts to raise him properly. Eventually, they will have no choice but to leave him to his life of wickedness, with its consequences.

God makes four primary judgments with respect to man: grace, reward, mercy and wrath. Each of these issues from God's loving and righteous nature, and is in response to the presence or absence of faith in each person, as well as what each individual is deserving of, in God's sight.

Grace is God's undeserved blessings bestowed on those in whom He finds a heart with which He can work. Noah, Abraham, Joseph, Moses, Gideon, Hannah, Mary, the twelve apostles and Paul were some so favored. Why? Because they were men and women who (some more quickly than others) hearkened to the voice of the Lord. Not only were their lives blessed, but so were all who were identified with them. These individuals upon whom the grace of God came were key players in redemption history as God worked with them to bring to pass His will. They were all flawed people, and undeserving of such divine favor on the basis of their moral quality. Nevertheless, God gave His grace based on His love and the faith He saw in the heart of each individual.

Perhaps the clearest example of the relationship between grace and faith is set forth in Romans 4:1-16, when God originally chose Abraham to be "the father of all them that believe" (Romans 4:11). He saw in Abraham's heart that he would believe His promise. Abraham did not deserve the promise— it came to him by God's grace. Then it was Abraham's trust in God's promise that allowed God to impute to him righteousness. This imputing was God's judicial act of grace.

Reward is God giving good things to those whose works merit them. As we saw in Hebrews 11:6, He is a rewarder of those who seek Him. Romans 4:4 sets the principle: "Now when a man works, his wages are not credited to him as a gift, but as an obligation." God is faithful to His Word. As He enters into relationship with His people, He is just and faithful to fulfill His side of the agreement. This "contractual" aspect of God's dealings with His people is in response to their faith in Him and their works for Him.

Ephesians 2:8 makes it plain that we are saved by grace, not by works. But there are many ways in which we as Christians are called upon to work for the Lord subsequent to salvation. [98] To the extent that work is required, the reward will be reckoned on the basis of merit, not grace. For instance, Paul refers to himself as a "steward of the mysteries of God" (I Corinthians 4:1), which is the same basic truth as stated in I Thessalonians 2:4, where he states that he was "put in trust with the gospel." In this relationship, Paul, like a steward, was expected to be faithful to his owner's interests, and the owner was to be faithful to take care of the steward's needs.

God is faithful and just, and we can expect Him to reward us for our works, both now and in eternity. The expectation of reward for his work was an important motivation in Paul's life (I Corinthians 9:18, 25-27, et al), and should be in our lives as well (I Corinthians 15:58).

When we believe in and confess Jesus as Lord according to Romans 10:9,10, we are saved. When we confess our sins, God forgives us (I John 1:9). If we give, we receive (Galatians 6:9, etc.). These are examples of contractual agreements more than God acting unilaterally to give unmerited grace, though grace enters the picture as God continually does "exceeding abundantly above all that we ask or think" (Ephesians 3:20). The Greek word for "ask" is often used in connection with a father and son relationship (Matthew 7:9, etc.), and implies confidently requesting rather than begging. God doesn't want us as His sons groveling at His feet begging Him for blessings. Rather, He wants us to ask Him, with confidence in His love and ability, to do for us that which He has promised (Hebrews 4:16). Because God loves His children, He is happy to provide for them in every way He can.

---

98. *Grace unto Works: The Christian's Reward* (CES Bi-Monthly Tape, Sep/Oct 1992).

To a great extent, our faith rests upon God's faithfulness to His Word, and therefore an accurate knowledge of it is indispensable. The integrity of the promises is determined by the integrity of the Promiser. Abraham judged God to be faithful to His Word (Hebrews 11:11). We too must let our faith rest upon the power of God to perform His Word. As the Scripture says, "Whosoever believeth on Him shall not be ashamed" (Romans 10:11).

Mercy is the withholding of deserved punishment. It is a judicial response that has meaning only if condemnation   is deserved or appropriate. A judge shows mercy when He feels there is some compelling reason to temper the punishment that should accrue to the offender. In Paul's case, he found mercy because he had persecuted the church "ignorantly in unbelief" (I Timothy 1:13). God must evaluate every man's experience and decide to what extent he has heard enough to believe and what he is accountable for. Once a person has heard enough, his unbelief is not due to ignorance, but is an act of his will. This becomes disobedience, and, in Scripture, it is associated with God's wrath (Ephesians 2:2,3; 5:6; Colossians 3:6; Hebrews 4:3 and 6).

Some will deliberately choose ignorance, thinking that it is preferable to understanding and accountability. They trust that God's mercy will continue to cover them while they persist in sinful behavior, because, as they are fond of saying, "God looks on the heart." However, it is precisely because God does look on the heart that He may not be able to keep on covering them. God has called us to grow up to maturity and responsibility (Hebrews 5:12-6:1). Ephesians 4:18 says that ignorance alienates us from the life of God. We are to replace ignorance with "truthing it" in love (Ephesians 4:15— literal). We are accountable to obey this instruction in God's Word, whether we want to or not, or think we are ready or not.

Every believer is probably at least a little aware of God having worked mercifully in His life to protect him from the full consequences of his sin. God may be able to cover us while we are maturing in a particular area of life, but if we choose to stay ignorant and if we keep sinning, eventually He must let us suffer the consequences of our sin. His desire is that we recognize the consequences of our sin and grow out of sinful patterns of behavior. A Christian's goal is not to be in need of God's mercy because of his sin and unbelief, but to walk in faith and experience His great grace.

Mercy is associated with other extenuating circumstances beside ignorance. God had abundant mercy and longsuffering toward the children of Israel because of the promises He had made to the patriarchs of the nation (Deuteronomy 1:8; Joshua 1:6; Romans 15:8, et al). He may also choose to show mercy when there is intercession by a mediator (Exodus 32:11-13). Nevertheless, there is a limit to the mercy of God, and eventually it gives way to His wrath.

We see three aspects to the *wrath* of God. The first is His decision to give up sinners to the consequences of their sin, no matter how severe (e.g. Romans 1:24-28). The second is God delegating the execution of His wrath to people who represent Him (e.g., I Samuel 15:1-3; Romans 13:4). The third is His direct execution of the punishment of sin (e.g., the Flood). Thus, not every Old Testament instance where God is said to be the agent of affliction and death is an example of the figure of speech *Metonymy of the Subject*. There are occasions when God acts at the expense of evil people to protect His own righteous interests. Each instance must be evaluated on its own contextual merit according to the principle mentioned previously— that God cannot act contrary to His loving and righteous nature and purposes. Thus is is imperative for us to recognize God's purposes in each situation, and overall, if we are to grasp the truth about who— God or Satan— is doing what, and why.

According to *The New Bible Dictionary*, "Wrath is the permanent attitude [and expression] of the holy and just God when confronted by sin and evil. It is a personal quality, without which God would cease to be fully righteous, and His love would degenerate into sentimentality...It is as permanent and as consistent an element in His nature as is His love." [99] One key to understanding God's wrath is to see that it is directed only at those who are richly deserving of it.

An example of God's wrath upon those who deserved it was when He sent the Flood (Genesis 7) to preserve the future of the human race. Man's wickedness had become so great that "every inclination of the thoughts of his [man's] heart was only evil all the time" (Genesis 6:5). Without the Flood, Satan's destruction of mankind was inevitable. [100] Another Old Testament example is the cities of Sodom and Gomorrah, which, in light of their "grievous sin"

---

99. *The New Bible Dictionary,* page 1341.

100. *The Sons of God of Genesis Six* (CES Bi-Monthly Tape, Jan/Feb 1993).

(Genesis 13:13; 18:20), God destroyed. Incidentally, both the Flood
and the destruction of Sodom and Gomorrah clearly foreshadow the
future destruction of all wicked men, as the following verses indicate:

> II Peter 2:5, 6
>
> If he did not spare the ancient world when he brought the
> flood on its ungodly people, but protected Noah, a preacher
> of righteousness, and seven others;
>
> If he condemned the cities of Sodom and Gomorrah by
> burning them to ashes, and made them an example of what
> is going to happen to the ungodly...

It is critical to understand that even though God did send the
Flood, He was not the *reason* for it. What was the reason? Sin. God
simply responded righteously to evil for the benefit of His people.
Had there not been such unbelievable wickedness, there would have
been no flood. It is a good and righteous act to destroy evil.

Throughout this book, we are endeavoring to clearly set forth
that God never causes those who love and obey Him to suffer or die.
God is always trying to help and bless His people. Occasionally that
means that He will work in such a way that evil people trying to hurt
or destroy His people will suffer or be killed. The Flood of Noah (as
stated), the hail on the Canaanites (Joshua 10:11) and the death of the
Assyrians attacking Jerusalem (II Kings 18,19 and Isaiah 36,37) are
some Old Testament examples of this. Eventually, God will show
His wrath against all evil, but He is waiting for the just and appropriate time to fully manifest His anger and indignation.

It is noteworthy that when God has worked in defense of His
people, His justice has been quite swift. In the Old Testament, God
did not cause the evil people He destroyed an extended period of
suffering. It is wrong to attribute to God the years of suffering that
many people go through when the Bible is clear that even God's
enemies have been swiftly judged. As we mentioned, the Flood and
the destruction of Sodom and Gomorrah are "types" of the future
destruction of all wicked people. God did not torture those whom He
destroyed, and neither will He eternally torture the wicked.

Man's Choice: Deliverance or Destruction

God's judgments of grace, reward, mercy and wrath are all vividly illustrated in the benchmark record of God's confrontation with Pharaoh that we discussed previously, and which we want to further pursue in concluding this chapter regarding God's judgment. God stated in Genesis 3:15 that He would bring into the world a man who would regain the Paradise that Adam had lost. In Genesis 12ff, God identified Abraham as the one who would father the race of the Redeemer. In Exodus, it is Abraham's descendants who find themselves at the risk of extinction under the tyranny of Pharaoh. It is obvious that although Satan is seldom mentioned in the Old Testament, he was very active in his opposition to God's plan to bring the "promised Seed" who would destroy him.

God had told Moses to warn Pharaoh that if he refused to let His firstborn son (Israel) go free, Pharaoh's own son would die. "I will slay thy son" (Exodus 4:23) is a simple statement of fact, and not a figure of speech. This cannot be the figure of speech *Metonymy of the Subject*, because Satan would have no reason to kill Pharaoh's son, especially when this would appear to validate what God had said. Why would Satan do something to undermine this avid opposer of God's people?

Some, like Calvin, have in fact assigned just such a role to Satan as the executor of God's justice (Let the record show that Hobbes did not agree with Calvin). What motive would Satan have for destroying the firstborn of Egypt? His role is to oppose God and strengthen God's enemies, in this case Pharaoh. It is more biblically rational, and more satisfying, to understand God meting out His own justice in this situation as He has declared, and backing up His words with actions consistent with those words, than to make Him like the chief priests and elders who arranged for the Romans to do their dirty work for them. The plagues upon Egypt were representative of God meting out His justice upon them, commensurate with Pharaoh's progressively more obstinate opposition to His plan. Correspondingly, each plague was increasingly severe, culminating in the death of the firstborn of all the families of Egypt.

Clearly, God was not unrighteous to kill Pharaoh's son. He more than sufficiently warned Pharaoh, clearly demonstrated His power through the plagues, and even declared by example to all Egyptians what they had to do to avoid this judgment: put the blood of a lamb on the lintels and doorposts of their homes. As for the rest of the Egyptian firstborn, their parents could have followed the example of the Israelites and saved them, but they chose to follow their misguided leader and thus shared in God's judgment on him. It was the choice of each Egyptian household whom to obey, and each reaped the consequences of its choice.

In like manner, Israel's fate was wrapped up in Moses, a "type" of Christ, and in their obedience to him. I Corinthians 10:1-6 shows that the Israelites were identified with Moses, who had found grace in God's sight. Because of Moses' relationship with God, all Israel was blessed with the same deliverance he received. All believers today are identified with Christ and will enjoy the deliverance that God wrought in His resurrection and exaltation, while the ungodly will be destroyed.

The same parting of the Red Sea by God resulted in both the final deliverance for the Israelites and the annihilation of the Egyptian army that pursued them. This record illustrates one aspect of the corporate element of both deliverance and destruction, as men follow their leaders into blessings or consequences. Each man has an ethical responsibility to decide whom he will follow, and this choice goes a long way toward determining the quality of one's life, both now and for eternity. Each man will be held accountable for his own choices, even those made by default, or as they were influenced by his leaders or culture. In the end, the question is: do we obey God, or men?

CHAPTER 8

CONSEQUENCES OF LIVING IN A FALLEN WORLD

The Reverberating Ramifications Of Sin

The Church Age in which we live began on the Day of Pentecost, as recorded in Acts 2. People were then for the first time born again of incorruptible seed, given the spirit of God, and became members of the Body of Christ (I Corinthians 12:13). From the Book of Acts until the Book of Revelation, we can find only five incidents that even seem to be God intervening in judgment (Acts 5:1-10, 9:8; 12:21-24; 13:11; I Corinthians 5:3-5). [101] Having highly exalted His Son Jesus Christ as Lord, God has given *Him* the right and responsibility to one day come again and *at that time* judge all men.

---

101. In Acts 5, both Ananias and Sapphira died when confronted by Peter. However, the Bible does not say that God killed them. It is reasonable to believe that when confronted with their sin, they died of something like shock or a heart attack, and that by revelation Peter knew ahead of time that it would happen. In Acts 9, Paul

But just because God is not directly intervening in judgment does not mean that people do not suffer the consequences of sin, as they always have since Adam. It is very important that God's people understand that such suffering is not God judging them, but is rather a consequence of disobeying Him, or of unwise decisions they made while living in a sinful world.

Take sickness as an example. Sickness can be due to the direct action of Satan, as with the woman who was bound by Satan in Luke 13:10-16. Sickness can also be due to the weakened state of mankind that is a result of Adam's sin. A person who dies of the flu could be a case in point. Third, sickness can be the direct result of a person's sinful behavior, as in the case of an alcoholic who contracts cirrhosis of the liver as a result of his drinking. Lastly, sickness can even be the result of innocent behavior, as in the case of a hemophiliac who gets AIDS from a blood transfusion.

By the way, have you ever heard it said that "AIDS is God's judgment on homosexuals?" One problem with that line of reasoning is that some heterosexuals (and babies) have it too, but that is not our point here. Why do many homosexuals have AIDS? Not because God is now judging them, but because of sin. Whose sin? Lucifer's, Adam's and their own. Despite all the current rhetoric to the contrary, including some from Christian circles, homosexuality is disobedience to God's Word (Leviticus 18:22, 20:13; Romans 1:25-27; et al), and therefore those who engage in it suffer the corresponding mental, emotional and physical consequences.

There is terrible suffering on the earth today. We daresay few human beings escape suffering, but those who suffer are *not* suffering at the hand of God! We trust this book has clearly shown that sin

---

could not see for three days, presumably because of the intensity of the light from heaven (Acts 9:3). Although the exact cause or nature of the blindness is not specifically stated in Scripture, it lasted only three days (verse 9) and apparently was not painful. The incident in Acts 12 about Herod Agrippa I and the incident in Acts 13 about Elymas the sorcerer both involve an act of God against men who were aggressively standing against the people of God. These two incidents do indicate that people who attack God's people are putting their health and life at risk. The record in I Corinthians 5 (which is similar to the one in I Timothy 1:20) about men being turned over to Satan refers to an action on the part of the Church to exclude evil and divisive men from the Church. It does not imply that God is actively intervening to harm anyone.

(Lucifer's and Adam's) is the root cause of suffering. Suffering is caused also by the ongoing activities of the Devil as he and his army of evil spirits attack mankind. Another cause is the compounded sin of people's disobedience to God's Word down through the years. Man's sinful nature has in large part led him to a self-centered lifestyle that disregards other people. A person who gets cancer, for example, may find that he has lived on top of an illegal toxic waste dump. A terrible tragedy, but one that is hardly God's fault.

Still another cause of suffering in the world today is people who live contrary to God's Word. We suffer mentally and physically from con men, thieves, robbers, rapists and murderers by the score. God has made it very clear in His Word that men are responsible for governing themselves. Our societies are run by men, not by God or by angels. Our judges, our lawyers, our juries, our police are all human beings. If we, God's created beings, do not see to it that God's laws for running a just society are enforced, then we suffer when the ungodly behavior of ungodly men manifests itself. There will always be some suffering due to the behavior of ungodly men, but it can be minimized if society recognizes and enforces godly laws.

God has done an excellent job of giving man laws that we can directly implement and also use as precedents, although for the most part our society today has strayed from them. James Jordan comments on modern American law compared to biblical law:

> Also, have our modern loose laws done us any good? Modern humanistic law is soft on criminals and harsh on the innocent. Biblical law is harsh on criminals and thus protects the innocent, the widow, the orphan, the poor, and the law abiding. [102]

It is no news that in America today the "wheels of justice" are grinding so slowly that they are practically in *reverse*. Many criminals are never brought to justice. For many of those who finally are, the modern American jail is an improvement upon their living conditions on the street. The Bible warns us that under such conditions, evil will increase.

---

102. James Jordan, *The Law of the Covenant* (Pub. by The Institute for Christian Economics, Tyler TX, 1948), page 28.

Ecclesiastes 8:11

When the sentence for a crime is not quickly carried out, the hearts of the people are filled with schemes to do wrong.

Prayer and faith go a long way toward insuring God's protection in this evil world, but the point should be clear. If society ignores God's laws concerning murder, rape, robbery, perjury, etc., and criminal activity abounds, then surely we cannot blame God when we are victims.

Furthermore, simply being *alive* in our modern world subjects us to a significant amount of suffering. The human body is not indestructible. It is delicate and temporal. By ignoring this fact, we produce a significant amount of suffering. We invent light bulbs and then become tired and run down because we stay up too late at night; we invent "junk food" and then have heart attacks; we invent watches accurate to a couple of seconds a year and then get ulcers worrying about being late; we invent motorized vehicles of great weight and speed and then somehow blame God when driver error or mechanical failure causes injury or death. Yes, there is certainly a lot of suffering in the world today, but God is not the one causing it.

Satan's Opposition

Satan is a parasite and a counterfeiter. Thus he and his purposes are actually defined by a proper understanding of God and His purposes. Satan's character and his purposes are diametrically opposed to God's. The Devil especially tries to undermine man's perception of God's goodness by afflicting the righteous while prospering the ungodly. His deception is geared to obscure both God's good works and his own nefarious schemes, and to confuse people as to the difference between good and evil (Isaiah 5:20).

Remember that it works to the Devil's advantage if he can confuse people about God's goodness. Let's take Mr. Noah Nuttin, who wrongly thinks that God is in control of both good and evil. Mr. Nuttin knows two people who sin in the same way (lying, stealing, adultery, etc.,— the type of sin does not matter). One of them suffers evil in his life and the other one suffers nothing, or worse, appears to profit from the sin. Is Mr. Nuttin confused about God? Absolutely.

Does Mr. Nuttin think that God is a fair and righteous judge? No. Does Mr. Nuttin have an understanding upon which his faith (trust) in God can grow? No. Score another run for the Devil. Mr. Nuttin would not have been confused about the situation had he been properly taught what the Word of God says about the real cause of evil, sin and suffering.

One of Satan's goals in his seemingly random affliction of people (and his corresponding distortion of God's written Word) is to make it seem as if God is judging and punishing people *now*. He wants not only to blind people to God's abundant goodness, grace and mercy, but also to convince them that God is unfairly, unpredictably and almost gleefully vindictive. From our perspective of contemporary Christian theology, he has pretty well succeeded.

The Urgency of Obedience

Although Satan is "the god of this age," he does not have *carte blanche* to afflict God's people. The more precisely we as believers obey God, the more difficult it is for the Devil to succeed in ruining our lives. Sections of Scripture like Psalm 91 make it plain that the effectiveness of God's protection of us is in large part proportional to our "dwelling in the secret place of the Most High" and "abiding in the shadow of the Almighty."

Satan tries to trick us into sinning (disobeying God) and by doing so leaving the umbrella of God's "protective custody." For example, when Satan was tempting Jesus in the wilderness, he twisted God's Word. By misapplying Psalm 91:12, he tried to get Jesus to do something dangerous and foolhardy that would have cost Him his life. He wanted Jesus to mistakenly believe that God's protection of Him was *absolute*, when it was actually *relative* to His faith in and obedience to God's Word. Nowhere does God guarantee blanket protection to Temple-jumpers.

If Jesus needed to remain in the will of God to assure Himself of protection, surely we do too. Sin in the life of a Christian is a primary cause of his vulnerability to spiritual defeat. If Satan can get a believer to act contrary to the will of God, it appears that this gives him an opportunity to step in and afflict him.

Satan carefully chooses his moments to strike, in accord with his goal to confuse people as to the difference between good and evil. He does not take advantage of all sin to correspondingly afflict each person who sins, because then he would eventually discourage sin, and his success depends upon encouraging it. He does take special pleasure in hurting God's people in order to make it seem that commitment to God does not result in blessings.

God does not kill people who love Him, or cause them to suffer. It is the Devil who causes death and suffering. God is righteous and just. If a parent, judge, schoolteacher, etc. were to act as God is portrayed by many as acting— punishing one person while letting another go free for the same sin— imagine the din of angry voices shouting "Unfair! Unfair!" And it *would* be unfair.

It is interesting that most Christians who write about suffering admit that it is unfair, or at least that it seems unfair. But their erroneous belief that God is the cause of the suffering necessitates a distorted rationale. Not wanting to point an accusing finger at *God*, a finger they would unhesitatingly and rightly point at people, i.e., Stalin, Hitler, Saddam Hussein, Snidely Whiplash and other perpetrators of heinous crimes, they are forced to say that "unfair" is really "fair" after all.

Philip Yancey's comment is representative of the confusion that exists concerning God's fairness:

> If, for the sake of a "test" of love, a husband subjected his wife to the trauma that Job had to endure, we would call him pathological and lock him away. If a mother hid herself from her children...we would judge her an unfit mother. How, then, can we understand such behavior...by God Himself? I offer no neat formula... [103]

The Word of God makes it plain that applying such a double standard to Him is unwarranted, since He is the epitome of a loving Father.

By doing things like afflicting some people who sin, and disregarding others, the Devil has confused multitudes. In Old Testament times, this confusion contributed to what came to be the popular belief that God, if He did not choose to punish someone for his sin,

---

103. Philip Yancey, *Disappointment With God,* page 249.

would instead punish the person's descendants. Job refers to this belief in his great speech in Chapter 21: "It is said, 'God stores up a man's punishment for his sons.'" (Job 21:19a). Recognizing that punishing children for a parent's sin while letting the parent go free is not justice, Job continued, "Let him [God] repay the man himself so that he will know it!" (Job 21:19b).

Jeremiah 31:29 and Ezekiel 18:2 also reflect this common belief in biblical times that God punished children for their parents' sins, as does the verse that we quoted earlier in Chapter One: "Rabbi [Jesus], who sinned, this man or his parents, that he was born blind?" (John 9:2). This verse shows that even Jesus' disciples were confused and were considering the possibility that God did punish children for some ancestor's sin.

Unless one understands the figure of speech *Metonymy*, it would appear that the Bible does indicate that God punishes children for their parents' sin. Exodus 20:5 reads, "I, the Lord your God, am a jealous God, punishing the children for the sin of the fathers [ancestors] to the third and fourth generation of those who hate me." But this is a great example of the figure *Prophetic Metonymy*. God is not actively punishing, instead He is prophetically warning of the consequences of Israel's disobedience. God does not punish the children of sinners! He even forbids that children be executed for sins they did not commit, as the following verse shows:

Ezekiel 18:20

The soul who sins is the one who will die. The son will not share the guilt of the father, nor will the father share the guilt of the son. The righteousness of the righteous man will be credited to him, and the wickedness of the wicked will be charged against him.

It is true that children often do suffer for the sins of their parents, in that such sins often allow Satan the window of opportunity to afflict them. By their sinful behavior, parents can open the lives of their children to the direct influence of evil spirits that cause confusion, sickness and even death. Sometimes the "consequences" children receive are very obviously related to the physical sin of their parents. Fetal-alcohol-syndrome and babies addicted to crack-cocaine are both examples of this. It can be documented that abusive tendencies, alcoholism and other sinful behavior tend to stay in a family for generations. But are these problems acts of God? No! If a mother is a drunk, she is sinning of her own free will. Her fetal-alcohol-syndrome baby is not God's doing. God is always trying to help and bless people in any way He can.

Again we want to emphasize that suffering or affliction is never, by itself, an accurate gauge of sin in one's life. The Bible shows that sometimes the righteous suffer while the sinful go free. That is not to imply in any way that there is no value to living a holy life. First, there is a Day of Judgment coming when the Lord Jesus Christ will judge every person according to his or her earthly behavior. Second, and most germane to our thesis, God does work to actively protect those who are trying to serve Him. Throughout the Bible, God is called the believers' "savior," "deliverer," "shield," "rock," "fortress," "stronghold," "refuge," "shepherd," "rearguard," etc. Although God cannot always totally protect His people from all evil, He is always actively working to "deliver us out of all our troubles" (Psalm 34:17). No doubt every believer can give examples of God's helping hand on his or her life.

God So Loved The World

Neither does the fact that God is not now intervening in judgment mean that He is not intervening at all. You often hear people ask, "Why doesn't God do something?" He has!

John 3:16:

> For God so loved the world that he gave his one and only Son, that whoever believes in him shall not perish, but have eternal life [life in the coming age].

God so loved mankind that He intervened in the course of human misery by giving to those who believe in Christ not only the solution to everlasting death and the guarantee of everlasting life, but also the possibility of victories in this life now. He gave His only begotten Son!

If you have been born again of God's spirit (Romans 10:9), you are no longer the legal property of Satan. He has no legal dominion or authority over you. You have been bought with a price, the blood of Jesus Christ, and you belong to Him. You are no longer dead in sin, but alive *in Christ*. You have been delivered from the judicial sentence of sin and its penalty of everlasting death (Romans 8:2).

The power of sin (the "old man"), however, is still in you (Romans 7:17,18), and certainly it is in the world. Although our old sinful natures will continue to fight against us as long as we live in the flesh (Galatians 5:16,17), obedience to God's Word can negate many of the consequences of our own sinful natures. For example, you can avoid the consequences of stealing. How? Don't steal!

We live daily in the midst of a raging spiritual battle, and our best shot at minimizing the consequences of Lucifer's and Adam's sin, negotiating the minefield of life and enjoying a meaningful relationship with God and Jesus Christ is to do what God's Word says, no matter what the circumstances. We are to reckon the old man dead and walk in newness of life (Romans 6:11). And we can do so, because we have a new, divine nature— holy spirit, the very power of God.

Adam's original God-given holy spirit was contained in his perfect physical body, which was designed to live forever. Each Christian has received the gift of holy spirit from Jesus Christ, the last Adam, *but* it is contained in our genetically corrupted, disintegrating earthen vessels. Thus Scripture refers to it as a "deposit" toward our future bodily perfection and everlasting life.

II Corinthians 1:18-22

But as surely as God is faithful, our message to you is not "Yes" and "No."

For the Son of God, Jesus Christ, who was preached among you by me and Silas and Timothy, was not "Yes" and "No," but in him it has always been "Yes."

For no matter how many promises God has made, they are "Yes" in Christ. And so through him the "Amen" is spoken by us to the glory of God.

Now it is God who makes both us and you stand firm in Christ. He anointed us,

Set his seal of ownership on us, and put his Spirit in our hearts as a deposit, guaranteeing what is to come.

Amen and amen. Having this guarantee, let us put on the mind of Christ and walk boldly in His steps.

CHAPTER 9

LIFE IS NOT A BIG PUPPET SHOW

Does God "Use" People?

I
t is greatly disturbing to see Christian people subjected to so
much doctrinal error about the problem of evil, sin and suffering. For example, *The New Bible Dictionary*, one of the more
popular conservative biblical resource books, states the following under the category of "suffering" (Hey, why not test yourself?
After reading each sentence, answer True or False):

In the Bible, suffering is regarded as an intrusion into this
created world. [TRUE / FALSE]

Creation was made good (Gen. 1:31). [TRUE / FALSE]

When sin entered, suffering also entered in the form of
conflict, pain, corruption, drudgery, and death (Gen.3:15-19).
[TRUE / FALSE]

In the new heaven and earth, suffering has been finally abolished (Rev. 21:4; Isa. 65:17ff). [TRUE / FALSE]

The work of Christ is to deliver man from suffering, corruption, and death (Rom. 8:21; I Cor. 15:26), as well as from sin (Matt. 1:21). [TRUE / FALSE]

(You're sharp! Five out of five— all true. OK, only one left.)

Though Satan is regarded as having power to make men suffer (II Cor. 12:7; Job 1:12, 2:6), they suffer only in the hand of God, and it is God who controls and sends suffering (Amos 3:6; Isa. 45:7; Matt. 26:39; Acts 2:23). [104] [TRUE? No Way! FALSE!]

"...It is God who controls and sends suffering"?! THEN WHAT'S THE DEVIL DOING? He'd be in an unemployment line somewhere, muttering, "Oh shoot, I was gonna make that guy sick." It is heartbreaking that so many sincere Christians believe what the last sentence from *The New Bible Dictionary* says, because it is just not true. Furthermore, it is in stark contrast to the other statements preceding it. If God made the creation free from pain, and if the work of Christ is to deliver people from suffering, and if there will be no suffering at all in the new heaven and earth, and if suffering is an intrusion that entered in when sin did, then is it not logical that sin, not God, is the cause of suffering?

Speaking of stark contrasts, have you noticed any in the Bible? For example, light versus darkness, life versus death, good versus evil, God versus the Devil. How could the same people who wrote the first five sentences we quoted possibly follow them with the last one, which says that God and Satan work in concert with one another? But *The New Bible Dictionary* was written by theologians, many of whom are, unfortunately, so "intelligent" that they have transcended the need to make sense.

Perhaps *Sports Illustrated* can clear things up for us. In its 1991 article about Magic Johnson having the HIV virus, and the promiscuity among pro athletes, an Atlanta Falcons player is quoted as saying: "I think maybe there was too much [promiscuity] going on. The Lord decided to stick a sense of urgency into this thing. I guess

104. *The New Bible Dictionary,* page 1148.

He just needed a hell of a good man to get the message across." [105]
Then, before the NBA All-Star game, Magic Johnson told the media,
"God chose me to get the HIV virus to show others how to handle
it." [106]

These pro athletes and *The New Bible Dictionary* are all implying
the same thing— that life is nothing but a big puppet show! In other
words, God is up there pulling all the strings, controlling what all
men do and what Satan and his spirits do. Not at all! God does not
need or use Satan to accomplish His purposes. In truth, His purpose
is to destroy Satan and end his dominion over creation, which one
day He *will* do.

We must be careful in what we say about God so we do not
misrepresent Him. For example, many Christians talk about how
God "used" them. We think most Christians who say things like that
actually mean that they chose to respond to God's working in them,
but the phrase itself can communicate something that is not true.
God never "uses" people, in the sense that He overrides our freedom
of will. We are not His blunt instruments. Rather, He works together
with us, ("for we are God's fellowworkers"— I Corinthians 3:9), and
in us (Philippians 2:13).

Some Christians may find a sense of comfort and self worth
in thinking that they are "used" by God. One practical ramification
of this erroneous idea is that it leads them, and others, to passively
wait on God to "use" them, rather than aggressively acting in
obedience to what God tells His people to do. Also, those who do not
think they are being "used" by God often end up feeling confused
and defeated.

According to *Webster's Dictionary*, the verb "use" can be defined in two ways. One is "to put into service or action." In order to
see that there is no scriptural justification to say that God "uses"
Christians (in the manipulative definition just referred to), there are
two passages that need to be clarified. The first one is:

II Timothy 2:20,21 (KJV)

But in a great house there are not only vessels of gold and
silver, but also of wood and of earth; and some to honour, and
some to dishonour.

---

105. "Where's The Magic?", *Sports Illustrated* (Nov. 25, 1991), page 152.

106. NBC television interview, Feb. 10, 1992.

If a man therefore purge himself from these, he shall be a
vessel unto honour, sanctified, and meet for the master's use,
and prepared unto every good work.

These verses contain an analogy between vessels and human
beings. The main points of the analogy are cleansing and readiness.
It is not valid to carry this analogy beyond these points to say that a
Christian is literally an object that must be "used" (acted upon) by
another in order to be of service. By his free will, a Christian prepares
himself so that he will be able to do God's work, and then does it.

The second section is:

Romans 6:11-13

In the same way, count yourselves dead to sin but alive to
God in Christ Jesus.

Therefore do not let sin reign in your mortal body so that you
obey its evil desires.

Do not offer the parts of your body to sin, as instruments of
wickedness, but rather offer yourselves to God, as those who
have been brought from death to life; and offer the parts of
your body to him as instruments of righteousness.

Note that verses 11,12 and 13 each contain an imperative. That
is, God is exhorting us to do (or not do) something. This makes it clear
that whether or not we obey is up to us. The way each of us "offers
the parts of his body as instruments of righteousness" is to choose to
do what God tells us to do.

Secondly, according to *Webster's*, the word "use" can also mean
"to carry out a purpose by means of." Only in this sense— that God
has entrusted Christians with the ministry of reconciliation (II
Corinthians 5:19)— could it be said that He "uses" us. Even then, it
must be made clear that He never forces us to do our parts. It is vital
that Christians use words the way God does in His Word. Not doing
so can lead to false doctrines and confusion in the Church. A
Christian who actually believes that God either "uses" him or does
not "use" him is less likely to act for God and more likely to sit and
wait for God to act upon him. This vividly illustrates the importance
of words to either limit or liberate, and why we are so concerned
about accuracy in doctrine and in practice.

In this context, there are some difficult verses in Romans,
Chapter Nine that need to be correctly understood. This chapter has

been debated for years, with those like us who believe in man's free will coming to a different conclusion than do Calvinists and others who believe in predestination. The latter group has often used verses such as the following to prove that God has absolute and total control over everything that happens on the earth:

Romans 9:20, 21

But who are you, O man, to talk back to God? Shall what is formed say to him who formed it, 'Why did you make me like this?'

Does not the potter have the right to make out of the same lump of clay some pottery for noble purposes and some for common use?

A book with some excellent insight concerning these issues is *God's Strategy in Human History,* by Roger Forster and V. Paul Marston. Concerning this image of the potter and the clay, they write:

"It is unfortunate that the fatalistic image brought to our western minds by this metaphor of the potter is almost the reverse of what would occur to a Hebrew mind knowing the background of the Old Testament . . . The basic lump that forms a nation will either be built up or broken down by the Lord, *depending on their own moral response.* If a nation does repent and God builds them up, then it is for Him alone to decide how the finished vessel will fit into His plan—and whether or not it will have handles! God alone determines the special privilges of a nation. Nevertheless it is the actions of the nation itself that determine whether it shall be built up into some type of 'vessel unto honor,' or broken down and destroyed." [107]

Does God "Permit" Evil?

To some Christians (though not enough), it sounds too hideous to say something like "God killed your son," when a child is run over by a bus. So they euphemistically say that God "allowed" the child to be run over by a bus. But can a logical mind make any distinction

---

107. *God's Strategy in Human History,* Roger T. Forster and V. Paul Marston, Bethany House Publishers, Minneapolis MN, 1973, pages 81 and 82.

between the two? Ours do not, and we doubt if yours does either. If God could have stopped it, but instead allowed it, He necessarily shares the responsibility for the tragedy.

Suppose you are sitting in a restaurant visiting with two friends, Bill and Joe. Bill sees a guy with a lead pipe in his hand sneaking up behind you. He turns to Joe and asks, "How's your family?" When you wake up, don't you think you will blame Bill almost as much as you blame the guy who hit you with the pipe? Who can truly love a God who causes suffering, or one who could stop it, but just decides to "allow" it to happen?

In the beginning, as we have stated, God decided to "allow" or "permit" the possibility of evil in order to make possible an unforced response of genuine goodness and love. If something contrary to His will happens, it is because *God cannot at that moment stop it* without going against His own nature. How could that be? We believe there are three very good reasons. First, because although He is the most powerful One in the war, His righteous nature requires Him to act justly toward His formidable foe, the Devil. Second, He cannot usurp anyone's personal freedom of will. Third, His justice requires Him to allow people to experience the consequences of disobedience.

To say that God cannot always stop evil flies in the face of many Christian people's fatalistic concept of "the sovereignty of God," [108] a phrase, by the way, not found in Scripture. To most Christians, this means that God is ruling over everything that happens, and is thus responsible for it all. Most Christians have also been taught that God

---

108. God is "sovereign" in the generic sense, that is, He does possess *ultimate* power and authority, and He will bring to pass His overall goal of a family living happily ever after. But He is not the sovereign ruler in the affairs of man to the end that His will is always done. For example, I Timothy 2:4 says that God wills that all men be saved and come to a knowledge of the truth, but obviously this is not happening. Robert Forster and Paul Marston develop this thought in *God's Strategy In Human History* (Bethany House Publishers, Minneapolis MN, 1973), pages 35,36. In *The King James Version*, God is never called "sovereign." A brief study of the words translated "sovereign" in the *NIV* will show that, considered in its theological usage, "sovereign" is not an accurate translation of *adon* (lord, master), *adonai* (lord), *shalliyt* (ruler, officer), *malkow* (rulership, kingship), and *despotes* (master, lord). Also, a brief look at a dictionary will show that it is quite possible to be "sovereign" without having absolute control over everything within your domain. Independent kings and queens were known as "sovereign," and we often speak of an independent country as being a "sovereign state" without thinking that everything done in it is under its absolute control.

is "omnipotent," which according to *Webster's* actually means "all powerful." [109] Obviously God does not have *all* power, because Satan also has plenty. We believe that most Christians use the term "omnipotent" to mean that God has the *most* power and therefore can do whatever He wants. Although we certainly believe that God is the most powerful, we do not believe He can always do whatever He wants. As we have previously stated, He has limited Himself in His Word as to what He will and will not do.

Despite how much we may love to sing the verses of "Joy To The World" at Christmastime, there are a number of *Scripture* verses that indicate that the world is not yet subject to the rule of the Lord. [110] For example:

I Corinthians 15:24-26

Then the end will come, when he hands over the kingdom to God the Father after he has destroyed all dominion, authority and power.

For he must reign until he has put all his enemies under his feet.

The last enemy to be destroyed is death.

It is obvious from the above verses that there is some "dominion," some "authority" and some "power" that is not yet subject to the Lord. Furthermore, it is obvious that death is an enemy of God, not a tool He uses, and that it is not yet destroyed. Another pertinent verse is in Hebrews chapter 10.

Hebrews 10:12,13

But when this priest had offered for all time one sacrifice for sins, he sat down at the right hand of God.

Since that time he waits for his enemies to be made his footstool.

---

109. "omnipotent"— God does not have "all" power. Satan has a great deal; angels and evil spirits have some; Christians have some. But *God* is the most powerful One in the fight, and that is why He will eventually win.

110. The last verse of the song says: "He rules the world with truth and grace, and makes the nations prove the glories of his righteousness..." Not now He doesn't, though He certainly will in His millenial kingdom.

Since Christ is now waiting for his enemies to become his footstool, it is obvious that at this time they are not under his subjection. But God *is* the most powerful and most wise one in the fight, and that means that human history as a whole will be resolved according to His will. The "whole" will be made up of the parts of human history— individuals— who chose to believe God's Word and do His will.

In regard to God's eventual victory, consider the analogy of a chess match between current World Chess Champion Bobby Fischer and the president of a high school chess club. Although the latter might capture a few of his opponent's pieces and perhaps, to an untrained eye, even appear to gain the upper hand at some point, the outcome is never in doubt. No matter what the lesser player may do by the freedom of his will, the master player always has a superior strategy that will result in ultimate victory. Likewise, God need not stoop to manipulating His opponent in order to achieve His goals.

Hearing this truth may at first cause some Christians great consternation, and even feelings of helplessness. Perhaps this is because they have actually trusted more in fatalistic predeterminism than in the love, power, ability and willingness of God to keep His promises regarding the present and the future. But wait a minute— think about the only alternatives:

(a) There is no God, your great-grandfather was a lizard and life is a "crapshoot." Good luck!

(b) *You* are God. Good luck!

(c) There is a God Who determines everything that happens. He is able and willing to both help you and hurt you, and there are no guarantees which He will do, or when He will do it. Good luck!

(d) There is a God who once made a Paradise for man and Who has guaranteed for those who believe His Word that it will one day again be so. In the meantime, He and His Son are far more powerful than their (and your) enemy and they are doing their absolute best for you each day. You have God's Word on it. You don't need "luck."

Which sounds best to you? When properly understood, this truth will for you result in greater love for God, greater hatred for the Devil and greater desire to obey God's Word.

Is God A Murderer?

If God is now in complete control of the world, then He is ultimately responsible for all human suffering— either by causing it or allowing it. Doesn't that make Him very hard to love? Maybe that's why you hear so many Christian euphemisms designed to take the edge off what, if people did to other people, would be called destruction of property, stealing, torture or premeditated murder, and would result in jail time. To say that God "called someone home" sounds so much better than saying that He "wasted" the poor soul.

Some typical examples of such misguided euphemisms are found in Roger Steer's otherwise inspirational book titled *J. Hudson Taylor, A Man In Christ*. Taylor was one of the most influential Christian missionaries ever to work in China, which he did between 1854 and 1905. Drawing upon Taylor's diary, Steer writes of his conversation with his eight-year-old daughter Grace, as she lay dying of meningitis: "Back at her bedside, he said to Grace, 'I think Jesus is going to take you to Himself. You are not afraid to trust yourself with Him, are you?'" [111]

After her death, Taylor wrote:

Our dear little Gracie! How I miss her sweet voice in the morning, one of the first sounds to greet us when we woke— and through the day and at eventide! As I take the walks I used to take with her tripping at my side, the thought comes anew like a throb of agony, 'Is it possible that I shall nevermore feel the pressure of that little hand, nevermore hear the sweet prattle of those dear lips, nevermore see the sparkle of those bright eyes?' And yet she is not *lost*. I would not have her back again... THE GARDENER CAME AND PLUCKED A ROSE [Emphasis ours]. [112]

---

111. Roger Steer, *J. Hudson Taylor: A Man In Christ* (OMF Books, Robesonia PA , 1990), page 208.

112. *Ibid.*, page 209. True, Gracie is not "lost." She will spend eternity with her father. Note how Taylor's feelings of sadness accurately reflect the teaching of Scripture: Death is an enemy and it stings.

Later, his 33-year-old wife Maria became gravely ill, and Steer writes that Taylor "could not pray unreservedly for her recovery." [113] How heartbreaking that with his misunderstanding of Scripture, he could not resolve whether it was God's will to heal his wife, and therefore he had no basis to pray with faith. Perhaps had he been able to, she might have recovered. After her untimely death, which left him with four children, Taylor wrote:

> From my inmost soul I delight in the knowledge that God does or deliberately permits *all* things, and causes all things to work together for good to those who love Him. He, and He only, knew what my dear wife was to me. He knew how the light of my eyes and the joy of my heart were in her... But He saw that it was good to take her; good indeed for her, and in His love He took her painlessly; and not less good for me who must henceforth toil and suffer alone— yet not alone, for God is nearer to me than ever. [114]

Taylor's journal entry leaves an obvious question: "Where is God's love for those whom He does *not* 'take' painlessly?" It must pain God to see someone who obviously loved Him so much be so misguided and so practically hindered by such debilitating error. How sad that it is *rampant* throughout Christendom. If the truth of God's Word were taught, such semantic sidestepping would be unnecessary, and the blame would be laid where it belongs— on the one-day-to-be-ashes shoulders of the Devil (Ezekiel 28:18).

What Is The Key To Divine Intervention?

Now then, there are only two alternatives. Either God some-times *cannot* intervene on our behalf, or He *will not* do so. There is only one place to find the will of God, and that is in His Word. There are many places in the Bible where we can look to see that God's will is goodness, wholeness, health, and life for everyone, especially His own family. One of the clearest sections is the four gospels— Matthew, Mark, Luke and John, which chronicle some of the life of

---

113. *Ibid.*, page 241.

114. *Ibid.*, page 245.

the living Word, Jesus Christ, who said He always did His Father's will (John 5:30; 8:29). As to Jesus' attitude toward human suffering, James Martin states:

> Of all the attitudes to suffering that the Bible reflects, that of Jesus must obviously be the most important; and it is plain that he did not regard it as punishment for sin nor as "sent" by God. He regarded it as something evil, the enemy of God and inimical to fullness of life, and so He sought to remove it wherever He could. [115]

In Jesus Christ, God intervened in the course of human misery, and through His Son He continues to do so.

Acts 10:38

> How God anointed Jesus of Nazareth with the Holy Spirit and power, and how he went around doing good and healing all who were under the power of the devil, because God was with him.

Did Jesus heal "all" sick people in the world? Of course not, but He did heal every single person in *His* world that he *could*.

Matthew 8:16

> When evening came, many who were demon-possessed were brought to him, and he drove out the spirits with a word and healed all the sick.

Matthew 12:15

> Aware of this, Jesus withdrew from that place. Many followed him, and he healed all their sick.

Jesus healed everyone who came to Him for healing. But look at this next verse, in which the word "there" refers to Nazareth, where He grew up.

Matthew 13:58

> And he did not do many miracles there because of their lack of faith.

---

115. James Martin, *Suffering Man/Loving God* (Harper and Row, Publishers, Inc., New York NY, 1990), page 43.

Why did Jesus not alleviate as much human suffering in His own hometown as He did elsewhere? Certainly it was not because His desire to do so had diminished. Rather, as the verse states, it was because the people there did not have faith in Him to do so.

The ministry of Jesus Christ established that God and His Son will intervene in your life every time they can. The basic biblical pattern is plain: *whenever and wherever God and Jesus Christ can help people, they do, and whenever and wherever they don't, they can't.* Thus it is imperative to understand, to the best of our ability, what God's Word tells us as to when and why He and His Son can intervene to help us, and when they cannot. We will see that this is primarily a *legal* issue, because, as we have stated, God is by nature a legal, i.e., a *righteous*, God.

Exercise Your Legal Rights

Remember that God gave Adam complete authority over His original creation, and that God backed up that authority with His own power, wisdom and might. But Adam, by disobeying God, relinquished his authority to Satan, who since that day has been the "god of this age." Satan has the legal authority over the world, including all the descendants of Adam who are born as citizens of his "evil empire."

However, God so loved the world that He devised a plan— another "Adam"— whereby, legally and righteously, He could regain dominion over creation and save all people who believe in this "last Adam" (Jesus Christ). [116] By the birth, death, resurrection, ascension and exaltation of Jesus Christ as Lord, God has made it available for all people who believe in His Son to become citizens in a new kingdom.

Colossians 1:12-14

Giving thanks to the Father, who has qualified you to share in the inheritance of the saints in the kingdom of light.

For he has rescued us from the dominion of darkness and brought us into the kingdom of the Son he loves,

---

116. *A New Race For A New Age* (CES Bi-Monthly Tape, Nov/Dec 1992).

In whom we have redemption, the forgiveness of sins.

Because the Lord Jesus gives the gift of holy spirit to each person at the moment of his new birth, each Christian is guaranteed a perfect new body and new life in the new age that will follow "this present evil age" (Galatians 1:4). [117]

Philippians 3:20,21

But our citizenship is in heaven. And we eagerly await a Savior from there, the Lord Jesus Christ,

Who, by the power that enables him to bring everything under his control, will transform our lowly bodies so that they will be like his glorious body.

That guarantee of holy spirit ("earnest"— II Corinthians 1:22; 5:5; Ephesians 1:14 KJV) is also indisputable proof to us Christians that, although we must live within the Devil's domain, he no longer has any legal authority over us. The gift of holy spirit we have been given is our passport to Paradise, to be honored as such by Jesus Christ in the future.

In the meantime, while living in this world, we must *know and exercise* our rights as citizens of "the kingdom of the Son." If we do not, Satan, who has always broken every law he thought he could get away with breaking, will disregard his lack of legal authority over us and treat us just like he treats those others who are under his dominion. Each Christian must understand his spiritual position in Christ, and live accordingly. What each believer is "in Christ" is made especially clear in Ephesians and Colossians (Ephesians 1:19-23; 2:1-10; 3:14-21; 4:7-16; Colossians 1:9-14; 2:10-15; 3:1-4).

The truths in the verses just mentioned are representative of the only solid foundation upon which a Christian can "be strong in the Lord," "put on the whole armor of God," "stand against the wiles of the Devil," and "withstand in the evil day" (Ephesians 6:10-17). Without an accurate knowledge of God's Word in regard to his standing as a son of God, a Christian has little chance to really see God's power manifested in his life.

Jesus Christ's perfect obedience unto death, and God's resurrecting Him and exalting Him as Lord are what has given Him the

---

117. If there were not a genuine future biblical new age— the Kingdom of God, there could be no counterfeit "New Age"— the so-called "Age of Aquarius."

authority and power He now has to intervene in the lives of those who belong to Him. Christ's victory is our basis to come boldly before the throne of grace and access His supernatural power by asking for divine help. It is also our basis to "ask in faith, nothing wavering" (James 1:6). In the next chapter, we will examine the biblical relationship between our faith and the power of God.

CHAPTER 10

KEEP THE FAITH

Faith Means Trust

Neither God's will nor the Devil's will is a variable. God always wants to help us, and the Devil always wants to hurt us. Thus the major determining factor and variable in the spiritual "equation" is *our faith*. There is a lot of confusion among Christians about "faith." It is very important to de-mystify faith and to become clear on what it is. Every Christian should want to have faith and to grow in faith. This is hard to do if one does not know what faith is.

What is faith?   In the New Testament, "faith" is most often the Greek word *pistis*, a word similar to thousands of other Greek words in that it has several usages or definitions. When, however, *pistis* is translated "faith" in phrases like "faith in God," "faith in Christ" or "have faith," it simply means "trust," "confidence" or "assurance." This is easily confirmed by checking any biblical lexicon.

For example: "...firm persuasion, a conviction based upon hearing" (*Vine's Expository Dictionary of New Testament Words*). "Conviction of the truth of anything; belief,...in reference to Christ, it denotes a strong and welcome conviction or belief..." (*New Thayer's Greek-*

English Lexicon of the New Testament). "...firm persuasion" (*A Critical Lexicon and Concordance to the English and Greek New Testament* by E.W. Bullinger). "It is the attitude of complete trust in Christ..." (*The New Bible Dictionary*). "In the New Testament, 'faith' is used in a number of ways, but primarily with the meaning 'trust' or 'confidence' in God" (*Hollman Bible Dictionary*).

It is easy to see why *pistis*, which means "trust" or "confidence," was translated "faith," since the English word "faith" comes from the Latin word *fides* which also means "trust" or "confidence." Everyone knows what it is to trust someone. We usually do not trust strangers, but if we meet someone, get to know him, and if he continues to act in a "trustworthy" manner, our trust in him grows. If, however, he breaks an appointment, lies to us or causes us physical or emotional harm, then our trust (faith) in him wanes. If we later find out that our friend never really did cause us the harm, but was "set up" to take the blame, then our trust (faith) in him is restored.

God is "someone," too. We understand Him primarily through the Lord Jesus Christ, but we can also see His characteristics in the Bible and in other Christians. As we hear His Word, do what He says and get the results He promises, our trust (faith) in Him grows (Romans 10:17). God says He loves us. God says He is light and in Him is no darkness (evil) at all. If we or someone we love is subjected to suffering or death and we atttribute that to God, our trust in Him is jeopardized at best, and very often it evaporates, which is understandable. Brother Andrew says it very well: "We can't be friends with someone who is totally unpredictable and unreliable. We have certain needs and expectations, and when those aren't met, it isn't possible to build a healthy or satisfying relationship." [118]

Thus it is paramount for a Christian to know the Word of God, because true faith can be based *only* upon an understanding of the character and promises of God. Faith is simply *trust* in what God says, and true faith issues in whatever response to His Word is appropriate in the situation. It is each person's "response-ability" to aggressively seek to understand and appropriate God's promises.

Sometimes faith is "leaping out" without specific revelation, and not even in obedience to some direct command, but in simple

118. Brother Andrew, *And God Changed His Mind*, (Chosen Books, Fleming H. Revell Co., Tarrytown NY, 1990), page 37.

trust in the overall character of God as revealed in His Word. This would be like confidently calling upon a good friend in a time of great need, because his previous actions have shown you that he is always willing to help you. Such faith is certainly rational, but it is also heartfelt and emotional. We see this in the life of the centurion (Matthew 8:5-13) and the Gentile woman (Matthew 15:22-28).

Sometimes such faith is manifest as in those who came touching the hem of Jesus' garment, crouching to get in Peter's shadow or touching Paul's handkerchief. None of these things had power in themselves, but we see that God honors the heart of a person and the faith he has in the power of God resident in His representative. In such cases, people judge themselves worthy of blessing, healing, etc., and receive it by the grace of God, independent of a specific promise from God to them.

God wants us to have faith in Him, but we cannot as long as we feel confused and hurt over the pain and suffering we think He is causing us. [119] We must come to the point in our lives that we realize that God does not cause death, sickness or suffering. Every Christian needs to get this fully resolved in his mind and heart if he is ever to fully trust (have faith in) God for deliverance.

There is another common misconception that can be cleared up by understanding that faith is trust or confidence. Pastors and teachers are sometimes frustrated when the people they are trying to teach cannot seem to grasp what they are teaching (sometimes because it is unscriptural and makes no sense). Many resort to saying, "You just have to take it by faith." How can one be expected to trust in something he cannot understand? How can one have confidence in something he cannot comprehend?

This "take-it-by-faith" line has caused at least two problems in the Church. First, false doctrines have not been revealed for what they are— false and incomprehensible— because people who challenge them are brow-beaten with "Take it by faith." Second, people who have doubts and questions are made to feel that they themselves

---

119. Please understand that it is possible to believe in God, i.e., in His existence, without having *faith* in God. A verse in James should help show the difference: "You believe that there is one God. Good! The demons believe that— and shudder" (James 2:19). A person dying of cancer may be angry at God, and feel betrayed by God. In such a case, he believes in God, but does not have faith (trust) in God, because he thinks God has betrayed him.

are the problem—that somehow they just do not measure up or have enough faith. Remember, "faith" is "confidence" or "trust." The next time someone tells you to "take it by faith," you can say to him, "No, friend, *you* explain it better so I can have confidence in what you are saying."

Remember, God did not create robots. He gives each man a choice as to whether or not to believe His Word. Man must cooperate with God to receive what He wants to give us. God decided to require something on the part of man, and faith may be thought of as the simplest thing God could require of man. Faith is man meeting a simple condition that allows God to help him. Faith is made possible by hearing God's Word, because faith requires an object, and God, via His Word, is the object of our trust.

Romans 10:17

Consequently, faith comes from hearing the message, and the message is heard through the word of [regarding] Christ.

Faith can and does *grow* (II Corinthians 10:15) as one learns more of God's Word and acts upon what he learns. Faith can also be destroyed, or as *The King James Version* puts it, "made shipwreck" (I Timothy 1:19).

Between A Rock And A Promise

Perhaps, at this point, a simple children's story will help to illustrate that faith is simply trust in something or someone.

Once there was a little boy and a little girl who lived in a deep canyon. Tall cliffs surrounded them on every side. The canyon was always full of fog and they could barely see their way around. When they wanted to go somewhere, they would just follow the deep rut worn by many others groping through the fog before them. All the trails ran in circles or into one of the walls of the canyon. The children had never seen the sun before. There weren't any rainbows or laughter or any fun things to do. They didn't know what it was to be happy.

One day the children wandered off the path and followed an old dry creek-bed. They stopped a moment to eat some moss;

that's all there was to eat on the damp canyon floor. Where the dry creek ended, they could barely see the remains of an old trail, obviously not traveled in years. They could hardly tell where the trail was now, but they could see it well enough to follow it a short distance.

Suddenly the girl tripped on something. "Whoops!" she cried. "Hey, what's this? Why look, it's a book!" So they sat down and gently opened the book. It was obviously quite old and looked like it had not been opened in a long while. The pages were mildewed and wet, but they could still read it and make out color pictures of a marvelous and beautiful land. Having never seen colors before— their canyon was always gray—they were very excited. The book described a land full of pretty colored birds and flowers and lots of fun things to do. They were thrilled to hear of such a place, even if only in a book.

But the little girl's face fell. "It's no use. We'll never be able to go there. That's just a book."

"Wait!" exclaimed the boy, "Look here! Here's a map of our canyon. It shows everything." He paused a moment to read on. "Here, look at this," he said. "This book says that if we just go to this rock right here and sit on it, an eagle will come and pick us up and take us out of here. All it says to do is sit on the rock and don't budge. Hey, what do we have to lose? Let's go find it."

So they followed the map and sure enough they found the rock exactly where the book said it would be. "See, said the boy, "the book is right so far. Why would it lie about the eagle?"

The little girl hesitated for a minute. "But what if it's not true about the eagle? Then we'll waste all that time sitting on the rock."

"But what if it is true?" replied the boy. "Then we're standing here gabbing instead of being on that rock. The eagle might come and we would miss him. If it is true, we are wasting our time standing here. We ought to be on that rock. Besides, what else is there to do? I'm sick of this canyon."

So they went to the rock, and waited and waited and waited. They craned their necks and peered through the fog looking for the eagle until their necks got sore. Finally the little girl broke the silence, "Maybe we ought to put out some food; maybe that would make him come quicker."

"No, don't be silly." replied the boy. "All the book said to do was sit on this rock and don't budge. There's nothing else the book says to do to get the eagle to come. There's no sense making up our own things to do to get him to come. Besides, we wouldn't be here sitting and waiting for him to come if we didn't believe the book. It was right about the rock, so let's just believe the book and quit thinking about where the eagle is coming from or how it's getting here. It'll come. If we have to wait forever, I'm not moving."

"Okay." she said, "Me too."

They lay back on the rock and began to daydream about the land of the book. It was so wonderful, so much better than their canyon. It was worth waiting for. They pictured themselves playing and walking in the sun in the new land, but finally they got tired and fell asleep.

They never saw the eagle coming or felt his gentle talons grip their waists and lift them off the rock. They awoke in the air beneath the graceful rhythm of his mighty wings.

"The eagle— he came!" shouted the girl. "He came when we weren't even looking. I just knew he would come!" shouted the boy.

As the eagle flew out of the fog, they saw the sun for the first time and tears of joy welled up in their eyes. The canyon soon disappeared behind them and the new horizon spread before them in a familiar sight. It was just as the book described.

"Oh, thank you eagle, thank you for taking us out of the canyon."

"Oh, you're welcome kids," said the eagle, "but you really have to thank the author of the book. It was all his idea. He'll be really glad to see you. It's been a long, long time since someone looked at his book and believed the promise that I would come."

They were amazed at how simple it had been to get out of the canyon. The children smiled at each other and laughed with joy. They couldn't wait to meet the author. They knew that he would be lots of fun. The book said so.

Faith Is Not A Force

The above story is meant to show that faith is trust in, and leads to corresponding action upon, a promise. Biblically, it is understood that the objects of our trust are God and the Lord Jesus Christ. We trust in them by trusting in their words. Faith is trust in a promise of God. Faith is not, however, the power that makes the promise come true. Rather, faith in God "accesses" *His power*, which is what makes His promises come true. Today, some Christians teach that it is your faith (some call it "believing" or "mental attitude") or lack of it that is the cause of everything that happens to you, good or bad. If you believe that, you will probably spend more time worrying about how little faith you have than dwelling upon God's goodness and willingness to help you, which is what will help your faith increase.

You will also find it very difficult to compassionately console others in time of tragedy. As we have seen in Chapter Six, it was error very close to this teaching that undermined the efforts of Job's "friends" to help him, because they believed the tragedy that had befallen him was somehow his fault. Their misguided appeals that Job change his ways did not comfort his heart, and, in fact, only compounded his grief.

In some current "Christian circles," a self-centered, what's-in-it-for-me, no-problems-if-you-really-have-faith, your-fault-if-you-do-have-problems teaching prevails. This dizzying doctrine leaves sincere Christian people with unscriptural, and thus unrealistic, expectations as to what the Christian life is. Often when something bad happens to someone with this mindset, he is shocked into confusion and gives up trying to walk with God, thinking that "it doesn't work."

To set the record straight, faith is not a force. It is not a power generated from within one's mind that either moves things around in the world, *or* makes God move things around. Faith is not something that manipulates circumstances, people or God. As we stated in the first paragraph of this chapter, faith is trust in and action upon what the Word of God says.

Scripture makes it clear that there is a definite relationship between our faith and God's action on our behalf, or on behalf of another for whom we pray. The fact that we may not be able to understand everything about this relationship should not dissuade us from trying to understand what God has revealed to us in His Word. Let us look at a few verses about this relationship:

Psalm 91:14-16

"Because he loves me," says the Lord, "I will rescue him; I will protect him, for he acknowledges my name.

He will call upon me, and I will answer him; I will be with him in trouble, I will deliver him and honor him.

With long life will I satisfy him and show him my salvation."

Faith is man's necessary response to God's Word if he wants to see God's power work in his life. Another pertinent verse concerns the woman healed by the power of God that was in Jesus when she touched His clothing.

Mark 5:34

And He said to her, "Daughter, your faith has healed you; go in peace, and be free of your suffering."

This is an interesting verse, because faith is not a force that heals. God's power is the force that heals. But faith is such a necessary condition that in Scripture it is sometimes put (as in the above verse using the figure of speech *Metonymy*) for the actual cause of one's deliverance. The literal meaning of Jesus' words to the woman was that her faith in Him had made it possible for God's power to work in her.

Consider also that Ephesians 1:19a speaks of "His incomparably great power for us who believe." So we can say that our faith "accesses" God's power. For whatever reasons, it is obvious that God has chosen to set up a cooperative relationship between Himself and His children. We believe that our prayers and our faith "authorize" God and His Son to intervene into Satan's worldly domain and help us. In any case, it seems clear that our faith in God's Word is the primary catalyst that releases God's power into a situation.

The Role of Miracles

The Bible is filled with examples of God's miraculous interven-
tion on behalf of His people. Because God has not changed, miracles
are still an important part of His relationship with people. The
manifestation of God's supernatural power serves to attract people
to His Word, builds our faith and brings glory to Him. Nevertheless,
sincere Christian people have been severely disillusioned about
God's willingness to help them when, in a time of tragedy, they
prayed for a miracle and it did not happen. It is pertinent to our thesis
to address the role that miracles play in God's working with us, so
that we do not blame Him if they do not occur. [120]

While it is God who energizes the miracles (Numbers 14:22,
Acts 2:22; 15:12, etc.), in nearly every case He requires someone to
"work the work" by faith in Him (John 9:4). In this way, Moses,
Elijah, Elisha, Jesus, the twelve apostles (Acts 2:43), Paul (Acts 19:11),
Philip (Acts 8:6) and others were the "secondary cause" of miracles.
It is understood that they did the miracles according to the will of
God and by His power. In such cases, the interdependent relation-
ship between God and man is clear. The following verses illustrate
this:

John 5:19

Jesus gave them this answer: "I tell you the truth, the Son can
do nothing by himself; he can do only what he sees his Father
doing, because whatever the Father does the Son also does."

Mark 16:20

Then the disciples went out and preached everywhere, and
the Lord worked with them and confirmed his word by the
signs that accompanied it.

John 14:11,12

Believe me when I say that I am in the Father and the Father
is in me; or at least believe on the evidence of the miracles
themselves.

---

120. Although we recognize that there are various types of miracles (such as miracles
of timing, angelic appearances, the casting out of evil spirits, etc.), for our purposes
in this book we are referring to the acts of God in which He supersedes the natural
course of events with His supernatural or creative power.

I tell you the truth, anyone who has faith in me will do what I have been doing. He will do even greater things than these, because I am going to the Father.

This reciprocal relationship between God and man is a truth that permeates His Word. This is particularly evident in regard to miracles. God gave man His written Word containing His "general" promises as to what is available from Him. It is now man's responsibility to believe what God has said, that is, to think and act according to this written revelation. Doing so orients one to God and enables God to give him specific revelation about a particular situation. Then it is again up to the person to believe that revelation.

Exodus 17:1-6 illustrates the truth of this reciprocal process. The people of Israel were "wandering" through the desert and they needed water. Moses, their leader, saw their need. It is obvious that he was a man who believed God's Word, as evidenced by his previous obedience to God. In the past year he had seen God's proficiency in dealing with water problems— the Nile River, the Red Sea and the water at Marah. Moses did not take matters into his own hands. He knew he needed specific instructions from God as to what to do about the current aquatic dilemma, so he prayed to God for help. God told him exactly what to do: strike the rock and water will come out of it. He did, and it did!

We believe that the following biblical record is another good illustration of God working with a man of faith.

Acts 14:8-10

In Lystra there sat a man crippled in his feet, who was lame from birth and had never walked.

He listened to Paul as he was speaking. Paul looked directly at him, saw that he had faith to be healed

And called out, "Stand up on your feet!" At that, the man jumped up and began to walk.

You cannot "see" faith. By revelation God showed Paul that the crippled man had faith to be healed and told him what to say to the man. Paul obeyed, and the man was miraculously healed. It seems clear that the process resulting in a miracle is not initiated by man. He cannot earn, will, or "squeeze" it out of God by his "faith." Faith, though usually necessary, is not sufficient by itself to produce a miracle. God's revelation and power must be present for a miracle to occur. Those who teach that miracles are virtually guaranteed and simply "claimed" by faith are setting people up to blame God, themselves or others if they do not occur.

The presence or absence of miracles neither validates nor invalidates one's doctrine, his ministry or his personal character (Matthew 7:22,23). The written Word of God, not miracles, must remain our only unwavering standard for truth. John the Baptist was a great prophet (Matthew 11:11) who manifested much faith and courage and yet did no miracles (John 10:41). Miracles, therefore, are not necessarily a part of every godly ministry or individual's life, although they might well be. As great a prophet as John was, he was killed in prison. Peter, on the other hand, was miraculously delivered from prison (Acts 12:5ff), as was Paul (Acts 16:26). Perhaps they had faith for deliverance that John did not have, but this is not possible to prove from Scripture.

Stephen was a great man of faith (Acts 6:5), and spoke the Word of God with boldness, yet he was murdered by the elders of Israel without being miraculously delivered. Many Old Testament prophets, great men of God, were persecuted and murdered (Luke 11:51). Hebrews 11:32-40 records many trials of the heroes of faith, and that many of them were not supernaturally delivered, yet they met their deaths with courage and faith in the resurrection. We must all recognize that our faith should be grounded first in God's character, goodness and love as revealed in His written Word, whether we see miracles or not.

In Scripture, miracles are inextricably linked to God's purposes for mankind. It is impossible for us to comprehend the myriad of variables He must consider in each situation. We do recognize that timing is one factor in the granting of miracles. For example, God could have parted the Jordan River (Joshua 3) without the priests bearing the ark having to first step into it. But by doing it as He did, God helped them and all the Israelites learn to trust Him. Similarly, God did not send Jesus to Lazarus (John 11) until four days after he had died.

Remember that miracles are examples of God overriding the natural laws of creation. Were He to grant miracles gratuitously, He would eventually begin to work against His own purposes. For example, Jesus fed the multitudes by God's miraculous power to meet their immediate need (John 6:1ff). However, rather than seeing this as an expression of God's loving care for them and desiring a deeper relationship with Him, the people saw Jesus only as the means to a selfish end— free food! (John 6:26). The Old Testament record of God's continual miraculous assistance to Israel (the Red Sea, daily manna for 40 years, pillar of fire, etc.) and their continuing hardheartedness toward Him shows that a miracle in itself does not necessarily engender greater faith in those who witness it.

Human nature being what it is, God obviously must consider many factors to determine whether the net effect of a miracle would truly benefit people and advance His purposes. There is a point at which man would tend to take advantage of God's goodness, and expect God to "cover" for him. No doubt many people who ask God for a miracle want it only in order to get them out of a jam, not to increase their faith and deepen their relationship with Him. For God to always accede to such requests would be analogous to a child whose parents do so much for him that it is actually detrimental to the child's maturing, and ultimately harmful to the relationship between the parents and the child.

Another important point to make is that in the Book of Acts there is a connection between the unity and mutual faith of the believers and the miracles they experienced. Likewise today, we in the Church need to pull together and help each other rise up to fulfill our individual potential and our collective calling as one Body in Christ. Doing so will make it most conducive for those particularly adept in the working of miracles to exercise their ability, to the overall benefit of the Church.

There is no doubt that God's working of miracles is a wonderful and awesome demonstration of His power and love. Miracles in this age also give us a window into the millenial kingdom of God and the new heaven and earth, when God's power will be fully manifested and all the effects of sin eradicated. Meanwhile, we see through a glass darkly and hope for the coming of that day, recognizing that in "this present evil age" there are some situations that God cannot correct, even though He does have the power to perform miracles.

Understanding the interdependence between God and man in the working of miracles helps us recognize the urgency of obedience to God. We are "fellow-workers with Him, and in order to do our part, we must know His love for us and His faithfulness to His Word.

We definitely have a biblical basis to expect to see miracles in our lives, but if and when they do not occur, we "don't blame God!"

Persevering In Faith

If you think you have faith, and you see no results, keep having faith, remembering that *faith grows* . You do not grow in faith by looking at how little you have, but by riveting your heart upon God and Jesus Christ and their love, power and burning desire to help you. This is very hard to do if you believe that God is the one causing you the problems in the first place. There is little comfort in thinking that God causes or allows suffering, and it is extremely difficult to trust Him for supernatural healing or deliverance if you think anything less than that He and Jesus Christ are fighting tooth and nail for you. No matter what the Adversary throws at us in life, God, His Son and millions of angels are always there to comfort us, strengthen us and help us. [121]

All God asks of us is to *obey Him*. He asks us to move forward into the spiritual battle, often in the face of extremely distressing circumstances. Why? Because He knows what is best for us *and* for the advancement of His purposes. As we will see, persecution and affliction should be no surprise to a Christian (II Timothy 3:11,12). Successful Christian living is not the *absence* of trial or persecution. Rather, it is continuing to walk with an awareness of the Lord's *presence*, according to God's Word, with the Hope of Christ's appearing always in mind. It is to adhere to Philippians 3:3, and "worship God in the spirit, rejoice in Christ Jesus, and have no confidence in the flesh."

What is ultimately best for us may not *feel* that way in this life. What is best for us may be in regard to *future rewards* we will receive at the judgment seat of Christ for standing faithfully amidst the trials and tribulations of this life, even unto death (James 1:12). God's Word does not emphasize total victory in every situation in this life as much as it does our ultimate victory in the age to come. In case you may be thinking of Romans 8:37 and saying "Yes, it does," let's take a look at that verse.

---

121. *The Ministry of Angels To Believers* (CES Bi-Monthly Tape, Sep/Oct 1991).

Romans 8:35-39

Who shall separate us from the love of Christ? Shall trouble or hardship or persecution or famine or nakedness or danger or sword?

As it is written: "For your sake we face death all day long; we are considered as sheep to be slaughtered."

No, in all these things we are more than conquerors through him who loved us.

For I am convinced that neither death nor life, neither angels nor demons, neither the present nor the future, nor any powers,

Neither height nor depth, nor anything else in all creation, will be able to separate us from the love of God that is in Christ Jesus our Lord.

Verse 36 is a quote from the Old Testament (Psalm 44:22), and the point of the reference is that because of the finished work of Jesus Christ, those who now believe in Him are "in Christ" and cannot ever be separated from Him and God, no matter what. Such was not the case in the Old Testament.

Verse 37 explains that, even in the midst of the trials and tests of verse 35, we are more than conquerors because, as verses 38 and 39 explain, we can never under any circumstances be separated from God's love. No matter what our response to such things, even if we fail to stand for God, we are forever *in Christ*, and in His love He has guaranteed us everlasting life.

Throughout our lives, we will be tested. Although by faith we can now be victorious in the Lord, our true victory is life in "the age to come," and includes the rewards that will be ours for what we have done for the Lord in this life. Understanding the truths we have covered so far will help us never to blame God for anything bad that comes our way, to look to Him in faith, and to persevere in serving Him, confident of our Lord's appearing.

CHAPTER 11

OTHER FACTORS IN THE SPIRITUAL BATTLE

Prayer: Taking Hold Of God's Willingness

We do not believe that faith is the only variable in the "equation" of life. A study of the Word of God shows that prayer, the intensity of the spiritual battle and the help of other believers are also variables that affect what happens in our lives. The prayers of God's people play an important part in the will of God coming to pass, because prayer is a catalyst for change— in people and in circumstances. No one knows how much sin and suffering could be avoided if Christians everywhere developed strong prayer lives. It seems that the power of prayer has been vastly underestimated. Prayer is not just reciting what someone else wrote; it is communion with God and the Lord Jesus Christ. [122]

Jesus Himself had an extremely powerful prayer life. He spent hours alone in prayer to God. Surely that shows the value and importance of prayer. Commands (not *suggestions*) to pray are found all over the Bible. "Devote yourselves to prayer" (Colossians 4:2), "pray continually" (I Thessalonians 5:17), "be...faithful in prayer" (Romans 12:12), "pray in the Spirit on all occasions with all kinds of prayers and requests" (Ephesians 6:18). And these are just a few. Paul knew that our prayers make a difference between success and failure in one another's lives: "On him [God] we have set our hope that he will continue to deliver us, as you help us by your prayers" (II Corinthians 1:10,11).

Many Christians have made resolutions to pray, but then quit when they did not see immediate results. Christ addressed this tendency: "Then Jesus told his disciples a parable to show them that they should always pray and not give up" (Luke 18:1). The parable is about persisting in prayer. Jesus gave us "the Lord's Prayer" to show us the essential components of proper prayer, and He taught us to be bold, persistent and specific when we pray.

Nothing is more vital to a Christian's cooperation with God than *prayer*. He needs us to become fellowlaborers with Him in writing "His-story." Through prayer, we can participate in events that otherwise would not have occurred. In his excellent book on prayer, *And God Changed His Mind*, Brother Andrew talks about how the false premise that God is in control of everything going on in the world, and its corollary fallacy that whatever happens is God's will, so dilutes a Christian's prayer life as to render it useless. He writes:

> The fatalist's attitude seems to reflect tremendous faith: "I refuse to question the will of God," he will say with pious humility. But does he actually mean that whatever happens in the world is all right with him— including war, famine, oppression, the breakdown of the family and society, the exploitation of the innocent and weak, and the degradation of all that is holy and pure? "If God allows it, there must be a reason," he will say, "and I can't hope to understand God's reasons with my small mind, so I accept what He does by faith

---

122. *Let Us Pray* (CES Bi-Monthly Tape, Sep/Oct 1993).

and praise the Lord anyway!" And ignorant listeners to this kind of talk will respond admiringly, "What faith!" [123]

The *truth* is, as he also writes, that:

The boundaries of evil are expanding every day, and fatalistic apathy is enabling those boundaries to grow because it offers no resistance. But Christians must oppose evil [which first requires a recognition of it and that God is not the cause of it]; we were born for battle! Every Christian is a soldier, a "member of the resistance" in God's army, taking part in spiritual warfare. The moment we lose sight of this, we become aimless in our actions and fuzzy in our focus. We forget why we were born, forget what we have been trained and equipped to do on the battlefield, and we die without knowing why we lived. Most importantly, we never complete the mission we were sent to accomplish. Score one more for the Devil. [124]

Faith in the Word of God is the only firm foundation upon which a Christian can build his prayer life. As Jesus stated in Mark 11:24, "...when you pray, believe [have faith]." Prayer and faith in God's Word go hand-in-hand. *Whatever God has promised in His Word,* we can, with faith, pray for. This is yet another reason why it is so vital for each Christian to know the written Word of God, because it is our basis to know what is available through prayer, and what is the right attitude to have when we pray.

Someone once said that "prayer is not forcing God's reluctance, but rather it is taking hold of His willingness." God's posture toward man is clear from Him giving His only begotten Son. Through the Lord Jesus Christ, God is always reaching out to give to His children "every good and perfect gift" (James 1:17). Prayer, based upon a knowledge of God's Word (which reveals His will and His willingness), is a primary way that a son of God can take hold of His many promises.

In this vein, the importance of each Christian's *free will* cannot be overemphasized. The biblical truth about the *rewards* that each of us will receive from the Lord validates God's appreciation of our individual response to His Word. He gives us credit for doing our

---

123. Brother Andrew, *And God Changed His Mind,* page 18.

124. *Ibid.,* page 23.

part as fellowlaborers with Him. Many Christians refuse to take credit for their efforts, and often reject other people's heartfelt appreciation, saying things like, "Give God all the glory." Scripture, however, clearly shows us that the way we truly glorify God is by recognizing the power He has given us, and using it to obey Him (see Romans 16; I Corinthians 16:17, 18; II Timothy 4:7,8; III John 12).

Angelic Warfare

Another biblical variable that affects our lives is the spiritual battle raging between the forces of good and evil in the realm beyond our five senses. Remembering from Ezekiel 28 and Isaiah 14 how much power and wisdom God originally gave "Lucifer" should help us to understand how formidable a foe we now have, and how diligent we must be in resisting him.

If you read Daniel 10:1-14, you will see that Daniel saw a vision from God, but he did not know what it meant, so he asked God to show him. Three weeks later an angel showed up. He told Daniel that his prayer had been heard when he first prayed, and that he had at once left "Angel Headquarters" to bring him the answer.

So why did it take him three weeks to get there, you ask? Because Daniel did not have enough faith? No, it was because "the prince of the kingdom of Persia" withstood the angel twenty-one days. Of course this "prince" was not a human being, but a high-ranking, territorial evil spirit. We do not know the details of their confrontation during those three weeks, but this account makes it clear that the spiritual battle raging beyond our senses may be the reason why certain prayers take time— a little or a lot— to be answered.

Daniel's attitude, however, is pivotal in this record. At the end of one day of prayer, he did not say to God, "Oh brother, you give me a vision and no explanation, and now you're asleep up there! I quit!" Then twenty days later an angel pulls in and says, "Where's Daniel?" No, it didn't happen that way. Daniel *continued* to have faith and look to God, and he did receive the answer to his prayer.

A verse in the Church Epistles illustrates this same truth.

I Thessalonians 2:18

For we wanted to come to you— certainly I, Paul, did, again and again— but Satan stopped us.

The Greek word for "stopped" was "used of impeding persons by breaking up the road [as by digging a trench across it], or by placing an obstacle sharply in the path." [125]

We see that, in the temporal realm, God is not totally in control of all circumstances. But He and His Son are right in there with us, working to help us go over, under, around or through whatever obstacles the Devil puts in our paths. In Acts 14 we read that Paul was stoned, yet through the prayers of the saints the power of God healed him. [126]

God is not a spiritual vending machine, where we just push a button and out pops what we need. Often we must hang in there for quite a while, as Job did, and continue to expect God's deliverance. In the context of spiritual warfare, it is significant that our heartfelt praise to God is a catalyst to help roll back the forces of darkness (II Chronicles 20:22). [127] No matter what happens, we have the ultimate victory— everlasting life in the age to come.

---

125. W.E. Vine, *The Expanded Vine's Expository Dictionary of New Testament Words*, (John R. Kohlenberger, Editor, Bethany House Pub., Minneapolis MN, 1940), page 551.

126. It is debatable whether Paul was actually killed or just stoned. The word translated "supposing" (KJV) or "thinking" (NIV) is *nomizo*, which means "to hold by custom or usage, to deem, think, suppose" (Thayer). A study of its 15 occurrences in the New Testament will clearly show that one cannot conclude from this word whether Paul was actually dead or not, only that the townspeople thought he was. In any case, whether Paul was unconscious or dead, the text does indicate a speedy and miraculous recovery. Conybeare and Howson comment: "The natural inference from the narrative is that the recovery was miraculous; and it is evident that such a recovery must have produced a strong effect on the minds of the Christians who witnessed it." [W.J. Conybeare and J.S. Howson, *The Life and Epistles of St. Paul* (Wm. B. Eerdmans Pub. Co., Grand Rapids MI), page 155.]

127. *Let Us Praise* (CES Bi-Monthly Tape, Nov/Dec 1993).

Timing Can Make The Difference

Another section in the Church Epistles shows Paul's tenacity and perseverance in prayer and action. Again Satan hindered him, but Paul's persistence did result in his eventually getting to Rome.

Romans 1:8-15

First, I thank my God through Jesus Christ for all of you, because your faith is being reported all over the world.

God, whom I serve with my whole heart in preaching the gospel of his Son, is my witness how constantly I remember you

In my prayers at all times; AND I PRAY THAT NOW AT LAST BY GOD'S WILL THE WAY MAY BE OPENED FOR ME TO COME TO YOU.

I long to see you so that I may impart to you some spiritual gift to make you strong—

That is, that you and I may be mutually encouraged by each other's faith. I do not want you to be unaware, brothers, that I PLANNED MANY TIMES TO COME TO YOU (BUT HAVE BEEN PREVENTED FROM DOING SO UNTIL NOW) in order that I might have a harvest among you, just as I have had among the other Gentiles.

I am obligated both to Greeks and non-Greeks, both to the wise and the foolish.

That is why I am so eager to preach the gospel also to you who are at Rome.

One thing we see in the above verses is that *timing* is often a critical factor in our accomplishing the will of God. Because of the configuration of spiritual forces that are beyond our perception, it is not always possible for us to "waltz along" on our mission from God. Sometimes we have to crawl through heavy artillery fire, and sometimes we must even stay in our foxhole for a while. The record in John 11 of Jesus raising Lazarus from the dead comes to mind.

John 11:6

Yet when he [Jesus] heard that Lazarus was sick, he stayed where he was two more days.

Why didn't Jesus go immediately? We do not know, because God's Word does not say, but certainly there was a reason. John 7:1-14 is also a most pertinent record, showing both the spiritual battle and Jesus' concern for the right timing in His actions. His brothers, who at that point did not believe in Him, urged Jesus to go up to the Feast of Tabernacles and "show 'em His stuff." Note Jesus' reply to them:

John 7:6-10, 14

Therefore Jesus told them, "The right time for me has not yet come; for you any time is right.

The world cannot hate you, but it hates me because I testify that what it does is evil.

You go to the Feast. I am not yet going up to this Feast, because for me the right time has not yet come."

Having said this, he stayed in Galilee.

However, after his brothers had left for the Feast, he went also, not publicly, but in secret.

Not until halfway through the Feast did Jesus go up to the temple courts and begin to teach.

Fellowship Is Essential

Another variable that affects our lives involves the way God relates to groups, nations, or corporate entities, and how everyone in such bodies of people can receive the consequences of corporate sin. There are times when what one person experiences is due to God's grace, reward, mercy or wrath on an entire group of which he is a part. There are many examples of this in the Word of God. All the Egyptians suffered because of Pharaoh's hard heart. Another example is in Joshua 7, where the army of Israel was defeated because of the sin of Achan and his family.

Although it may not at first seem "fair" that a person would be dealt with by God as part of a group, rather than on his or her own merits, the Bible and history clearly indicate that this happens. This is one of the main reasons why Christians are to be concerned about "social evils," and work to keep society free from sin. Certain cultures have been and are much more God-oriented and accepting of spiritual truth than are others. That is one reason why God exhorts believers to pray for community leaders that the laws they make are conducive to Christians being free to live according to the dictates of God's Word (I Timothy 2:1ff).

In the category of how God relates to groups of people is something we will call "community faith," that is, the mutual faith of individual Christians who associate with one another. Jesus alluded to this when He spoke of two or three believers gathered together in His name (Matthew 18:20). Every Christian knows that some churches or fellowships are "hot" and see great movements of God on a regular basis, while other churches are "cold" and have not seen God move powerfully in years. The fervent prayers of a group of Christians who are "of one accord" are synergistic, that is, greater than the sum of their individual prayers. In the spiritual battle, there are times when we as Christians must "link arms" with other brethren in order to be victorious (Acts 4:23-33).

When Jesus Christ walked among people, the love and power in His words and deeds generated great faith in many people. In other words, Jesus Himself was a compelling object of faith. Today, Jesus is not living among us in person. But, via the gift of holy spirit, He does live within each Christian. As each of us comes to know the Lord Jesus and exercises His supernatural power resident within us, and as we speak the truth in love one to another, we provide visible examples of God's goodness, and thus help others grow in faith. This is one reason why dynamic Christian fellowship based upon the truth of God's Word is indispensable, as the following verses show. Without it, many believers remain weak in faith.

Hebrews 10:23-25

Let us hold unswervingly to the hope we profess, for he who promised is faithful.

And let us consider how we may spur one another on toward love and good deeds.

Let us not give up meeting together, as some are in the habit of doing, but let us encourage one another— and all the more as you see the Day approaching.

To do what the above verses exhort us to do, we must first be learning the Lordship of Jesus Christ in our individual lives— by prayer, reading the Word and reaching out to others in His stead, among other things. As we do this, our confidence in who we are in the Lord, our awareness of our own function in the Body of Christ and our zeal to diligently carry it out all grow.

Second, we must get together with other Christians, and continue to do so on a regular basis, and in a variety of ways. Third, whenever we do so, our attitude should be, "What can I do to bless someone?" The more secure you are in Christ, the more you are willing to be vulnerable in reaching out to others via loving doctrine, reproof or correction. The more real the Lord Jesus is to you, the more confident you are that He will work in you to help your brethren. This is why fellowship and faith are in one way mutually dependent. It is much more difficult to grow in faith if you are not actively involved in a Christian fellowship that is based upon the truth of God's Word, practiced in love. [128]

128. In fact, the wrong kind of fellowship can work against your faith and your love for the Lord. Paul wrote to the church at Corinth "...I have no praise for you, for your meetings do more harm than good" (I Corinthians 11:17).

CHAPTER 12

THE FATHERLY DISCIPLINE OF GOD

Father Knows Best

The erroneous teaching that God causes suffering (other than in His righteous judgment of evil people) has helped Satan promulgate one of his favorite and most effective lies— that God is at best not fair, and at worst downright mean. Of course, that's what he (as "Lucifer") originally thought! Too many believers throughout history have fallen victim to that attitude, and we see an Old Testament example of this when the children of Israel were wandering in the wilderness after their exodus from Egypt.

Had they obeyed God, they could have made it into the Promised Land in eleven days (Deut. 1:2). Instead, they spent 40 years wandering in the wilderness. In theological terms, we call that "lost." At one point, the Israelites pitched camp at a place where there was no water. Forgetting God's ability when it comes to water (the bloody Nile, the Red Sea and His purifying the water at Marah), they began complaining and said, "Is the Lord among us, or not?" (Exodus 17:1-7). This doubt of God's protective care and custody is referred to in verse seven as "tempting God."

Many a believer has wavered in faith when confronted by a challenging obstacle. But our faith today should never be shaken by thinking that God is not with us. Both He and His Son Jesus Christ are with us, and they are also doing all they can to help us. How do we know? The Bible tells us so. True faith means adhering to the testimony of the written Word as the final authority, even when one's senses, because of their perception of need, lack or want, are clamoring that you do otherwise.

At the end of their forty years in the wilderness, Moses spoke to the Israelites.

Deuteronomy 8:1-4

Be careful to follow every command I am giving you today, so that you may live and increase and may enter and possess the land that the Lord promised on oath to your forefathers.

Remember how the Lord your God led you all the way in the desert these forty years, to humble you and to test you in order to know what was in your heart, whether or not you would keep his commands.

He humbled you, causing you to hunger [129] and then feeding you with manna, which neither you nor your fathers had known, to teach you that man does not live on bread alone but on every word that comes from the mouth of the Lord.

Your clothes did not wear out and your feet did not swell during these forty years.

We see that despite their obstinance, God had not forsaken them, and had in fact been helping them the whole time. The reason

---

129. The people were not starving or even "hungry." They had all the manna they could eat, but they were allowed to be "hungry" for the foods they had enjoyed in Egypt. ["We remember the fish we ate in Egypt at no cost— also the cucumbers, melons, leeks, onions and garlic. But now we have lost our appetite; we never see anything but this manna!" (Numbers 11:5,6)]. Note that God says in Deuteronomy 8:3 that the manna was to show them that man lives by the Word of God, not "delicious food" (and the pagan parties where it was consumed).

it took forty years before they could enter the Promised Land was that God had to wait until the faithless generation died off. Why? Because He knew that in their spiritually anemic condition they would have been no match for the evil inhabitants of Canaan, and that had they been wiped out, the bloodline required to bring to pass the Redeemer would have been destroyed. God *always* has His people's best interests at heart.

Deuteronomy 8:5-6

Know then in your heart that as a man disciplines his son, so the Lord your God disciplines you.

Observe the commands of the Lord your God, walking in his ways and revering him.

Although the description of God as a father is minimal in the Old Testament compared to the New, where countless times God is called "Father," here God uses the analogy of a father and a child to help His people understand how He was working with them. What was his goal? Their immediate preservation and their long-term benefit.

Deuteronomy 8:16

He gave you manna to eat in the desert, something your fathers had never known, to humble and to test you so that in the end it might go well with you.

A father sits down his three-year-old daughter and explains to her how she is to behave, and that if she is disobedient she will be disciplined, in love and in a way appropriate to the degree of her "sin." He tells her that she, not he, will always determine whether or not she is punished. He says that she can choose whether to obey or disobey, and in either case he will respond righteously. She says, "Huh?"

Another father walks up to his three-year-old daughter and belts her in the mouth for no apparent reason. The neighbors find out. What do they scream? "Child abuse!" And rightly so. Unfortunately, that is exactly how much of Christianity has represented, or actually mis-represented, God in His dealings with mankind in general, and even with His own children.

One reason Satan works so hard to destroy the godly concept of a family is so that when people hear the word "Father," it will bring to their minds memories of indifference or abuse. His goal is that when such people are presented with the Gospel, and hear that *God* wants to be their Father, they say, "No thanks! My human father could only kick me across the room! *God* is liable to put me in orbit!" In light of our current context— the fatherly discipline of God— think about how *you* treat your children, and ask yourself if you would ever do to them what countless Christian people say God does to His children. We doubt that you would.

Jesus Christ, The Son Of The Father

In the New Testament, Jesus Christ made known God as a loving Father, and exemplified for us how to trust God no matter how bad circumstances may appear. Knowing that *God* is also our *Father* helps us understand how He works with us to help us do His will, for our ultimate benefit.

Hebrews 12:1-4

Therefore, since we are surrounded by such a great cloud of witnesses, let us throw off everything that hinders and the sin that so easily entangles, and let us run with perseverance the race marked out for us.

Let us fix our eyes on Jesus, the author and perfecter of our faith, who for the joy set before him endured the cross, scorning its shame, and sat down at the right hand of the throne of God.

Consider him who endured such opposition from sinful men, so that you will not grow weary and lose heart.

In your struggle against sin, you have not yet resisted to the point of shedding your blood.

In Chapter Three, we quoted Hebrews 5:7-9 from *The Moffatt Bible.* At this point, these verses are once again pertinent.

Hebrews 5:7-9

During the days of Jesus' life on earth, he offered up prayers and petitions with loud cries and tears to the one who could save him from death, and he was heard because of his reverent submission.

Although he was a son, he learned obedience from what he suffered

And, once made perfect, he became the source of eternal salvation for all who obey him.

In those verses it is clear that the cross of Calvary was the Son of God's greatest challenge, and that His Father had prepared Him for it by helping Him to overcome previous, lesser challenges. Many of these were also in the category of "opposition from sinful men" as in verse three above. Hebrews 12:1-4 lays the groundwork for the ensuing verses.

Hebrews 12:5,6 (KJV)

And ye have forgotten the exhortation which speaketh unto you as unto children, My son, despise not thou the chastening of the Lord, nor faint when thou art rebuked of him:

For whom the Lord loveth he chasteneth, and scourgeth [130] every son whom he receiveth.

At this point we could cast away the moorings of context, lexical aids and sound biblical exegesis and zoom off into the stratosphere of theological speculation, a realm where, as it was once said, "words, shorn at last of their semantic burden, pirouette and regroup in combinations hitherto undreamed of." For example: "Yes, brother, that athlete's foot you have is the *chastening of the Lord!*"

Hold it, let's stay anchored in the context. Why do verses 1-4 precede verses 5ff? The father-child analogy of verses 5ff is relevant both to Jesus and to us. Jesus was our example. He refused to allow the opposition of sinners to make Him faint in His mind, that is, to forget God's fatherly exhortation. It is vital to note that the Greek word for "chastening" in verse 5 is *paideia*, which means "the whole training and education of children which relates to the cultivation of

---

130. The Greek word *mastigoo* ("scourgeth") literally means "to whip." *Kittel's Theological Dictionary of the New Testament*, Vol. IV (Eerdmans, Grand Rapids, MI, 1967), p. 518 reads: "The word is used figuratively in Hebrews 12:6, and means 'to impart corrective punishment.'" Used with the word *paideuo*, this verse is importing the image of a first-century schoolroom, where teachers employed corporal punishment to maintain discipline in the classroom. Even this does not in any way imply the infliction of any real harm or injury, or a desire on the part of the instructor to do so. No good parent would allow any real harm to come to his child in school, either then or now. So it is with our heavenly Father. He most certainly reproves and corrects us, and does all He can in order to get our attention and get the point across.

mind and morals, and employs for this purpose now commands and admonitions, now reproof and punishment." [131]

Remember that *love* (vs. 6) is the reason for God's instruction of His children. In the following pages, we will go into detail about the father-child relationship set forth in Hebrews 12:5,6. We will also consider what true discipline is, and see some biblical examples of the "chastening of the Lord."

A Father And His Children

How does a godly father deal with his children? Loving each one with the same degree of fervent love, he recognizes their differences in age, ability and experience. First he instructs each child as to how to do a certain thing. Then he tests him by asking him to do it. If the child disobeys or does it wrong, he corrects him. When the child gets it right, the father rewards him appropriately and in light of the "big picture" of the whole family. This process is known as "discipline," and it is exactly how God our Father works with us.

You can see that the word "disciple" is closely related to the word "discipline." Many people today have an unnecessarily negative connotation of "discipline," perhaps because their fathers abused them and called it "discipline." In Scripture, the Greek word translated "disciple" means "a learner; one who follows both the teacher and the teaching." [132] Does genuine parental discipline include breaking a kid's arm when he reaches rudely across the dinner table

---

131. *Thayer's Greek-English Lexicon of the New Testament* (Baker Book House, Grand Rapids MI, 1977), page 473. The Greek word for "child" is *pais*. *Paideia* (a noun) comes from *pais*. The verb is *paideuo*— to train or instruct. *Kittel's*, Vol. 5, page 621, says of *paideia*: "The relation between father and son is shown to be a moral one by the education, discipline and correction which the father accords to the son in responsible love." We are aware that, in the Greek language, *paideuo* has a range of meanings and that Greek teachers did, on occasion, use corporal punishment on their students, as have countless educators through the years. This meaning gets carried over into the trial of Christ, where the word *paideuo* refers to the beating that Pilate wanted to give Christ so that he would learn to behave himself (Luke 23:22). It should be obvious that the example of Pilate does not involve a father with his children.

132. E.W. Bullinger, *Lexicon*, page 146.

for the last brownie? Of course not. Such extreme and unwarranted cruelty would today be called "child abuse," and biblically it could be classified as "provoking children to wrath." Ephesians 6:4 tells parents not to do this, but on the contrary to "bring them up in the nurture [*paideia*] and admonition of the Lord."

In any language, some words change in meaning over the years, and usually they acquire a more negative connotation. Today the English word "chastening" leaves a bad taste in most people's mouths, but consider this fabulous definition from the 1841 Webster's Dictionary: "guidance by kind correction to prevent repetition of faults and reclaim the offender." That is exactly how God, our wonderful Father, works with us as His children. *Never* is His "chastening" via sickness, affliction or tragedy.

In essence, we are talking about the difference between *punishment* and *discipline*. Punishment focuses on past mistakes, while discipline focuses on correct future behavior. It is very important to correctly understand "the chastening of the Lord." If one believes that the chastening of the Lord means that God causes suffering in his life, then, as has already been stated, his trust (faith) in God's love and help in times of trouble is undermined. We have seen that *paideia* ("chastening") means training and instruction, and this is clearly set forth in a number of verses.

For example, in II Timothy 3:16, it says that the Scriptures are given for "instruction" [*paideia*] in righteousness." Acts 7:22 says Moses "was learned [*paideuo*] in all the wisdom of Egypt." Acts 22:3 says Paul was "taught [*paideuo*] according to the perfect manner of the law." II Timothy 2:25 says God's servants are to "instruct" (*paideuo*) those that oppose.

It is unfortunate, and it has actually helped the Devil's cause, that *paideia* and *paideuo* are so often translated as "chastening." No loving earthly father would cause his children the horrible suffering experienced by so many people today. To say that God's "training and instruction" (His *paideia*) is blindness, cancer, car wrecks, Alzheimers, AIDS, starvation, etc., is a slap in the face to God, who over and over in His Word has said that these things are the results of the corrupting influence of sin.

The point is clear: The Devil wants people to believe that God causes pain and suffering, so that he can destroy their love for and faith (trust) in God. The unfortunate translation of *paideia* as "chastening" helps paint that picture. God, meanwhile, actually says that He "educates and instructs" His children as any loving father would do— by challenging, testing, encouraging and reproving them in a loving way with the child's best interests in mind.

In regard to the "chastening" of the Lord, it is appropriate at this point to remind the reader of the difference between the Old Testament and the New Testament.

Judges 2:20-22

Therefore the Lord was very angry with Israel and said, "Because this nation has violated the covenant that I laid down for their forefathers and has not listened to me,

I will no longer drive out before them any of the nations Joshua left when he died.

I will use them to test Israel and see whether they will keep the way of the Lord and walk in it as their forefathers did."

Here we see another example of the figure *Prophetic Metonymy*. God did not literally "use" Gentiles against Israel, but rather foretold that Gentiles would be a test to Israel. Numerous Old Testament verses seem to indicate that God "used" other nations to afflict Israel in order to teach them to obey Him. Such circumstantial "discipline" was not, however, God literally empowering these pagan nations against His people. It was due to Israel's failure to obey God, and their subsequent vulnerability to others who were actually inspired by Satan.

What are some New Testament examples of "the chastening of the Lord?" In Matthew 16:23, Jesus sternly rebuked Peter: "Get thee behind me, Satan!" In Acts 10:15, God gently corrected Peter. In Acts 16:6,7, God, by revelation, said "No" to Paul and his pals. In Galatians 2:11-14, Paul by God's direction heartily reproved his Christian brother Peter. As one radio Bible teacher once said, "God's 'No's' are part of His 'Yes!'" In other words, sometimes when we ask God for something, He says "No," because He knows what we have asked for is not best for us at that time. God can certainly "close doors" as well as open them for us, *but He does not slam them on our fingers*!

An important point to note in these records is that in each of the above cases, those "chastened" responded by correcting their attitude and behavior. In Acts 5:1-11, Ananias and Sapphira could have responded in the same way. Instead, they did not repent of their sin and were apparently overcome with terror and dropped dead. In any case, the Bible does not say that God killed them, because He did not. If God killed every believer who was financially dishonest, we daresay the ranks of the Church would be considerably thinned.

There are many other biblical accounts where those whom God corrected did not respond accordingly. For example, King Saul did not change when he was reproved by Samuel for his disobedience (I Samuel 15), and both Saul and his subjects suffered much due to his hardness of heart. II Chronicles 16 records that King Asa of Judah became so enraged at the reproof delivered by a prophet that he put the prophet in jail and brutally oppressed some of his own subjects. Later on, when Asa was sick, he would not ask God for healing.

"Chastening" And Change

As humans, we all sin, and it is always the best thing for us if we are stopped and brought back to the right way by someone's loving reproof and correction. This is rarely pleasant. When someone confronts us about our sin, we are usually pained by sorrow and shame. In such cases, the mental anguish we experience *feels* a lot like that which tragic circumstances may generate in us. The difference is that "godly sorrow" can and should be a catalyst for change (repentance), because light has made manifest darkness, and shown us a way out. In contrast, "worldly sorrow" leaves us feeling like victims of circumstances beyond our control, and drains our lives.

Paul vividly expresses this truth in one of his two epistles to the Corinthians, much of which is his confronting them about their sins.

II Corinthians 7:8-10

Even if I caused you sorrow by my letter, I do not regret it. Though I did regret it— I see that my letter hurt you, but only for a little while—

Yet now I am happy, not because you were made sorry, but because your sorrow led you to repentance. For you became sorrowful as God intended and so were not harmed in any way by us.

Godly sorrow brings repentance that leads to salvation and leaves no regret, but worldly sorrow brings death.

These are tremendous verses, and they contain great truths regarding genuine godly sorrow. Note that the stinging reproof Paul gave to the Corinthians "hurt" them in that it caused sorrow, but not sorrow that drained their strength and faith. Rather it was godly sorrow that led to a positive change in their behavior.

Earlier in this chapter, we looked at Hebrews 12:1-6. Hebrews 12 then goes on to exhort us as God's children not to run away from God's fatherly correction and be like someone with no father, but to receive His discipline, knowing that it is rendered in love for our benefit.

Hebrews 12:7-11

Endure hardship as discipline; God is treating you as sons. For what son is not disciplined by his father?

If you are not disciplined (and everyone undergoes discipline), then you are illegitimate children and not true sons.

Moreover, we have all had human fathers who disciplined us and we respected them for it. How much more should we submit to the Father of our spirits and live!

Our fathers disciplined us for a little while as they thought best; but God disciplines us for our good, that we may share in his holiness.

No discipline seems pleasant at the time, but painful. Later on, however, it produces a harvest of righteousness and peace for those who have been trained by it.

Because of the great profit in discipline and godly sorrow— a "harvest of righteousness and peace"— God then goes on in verses 12 and 13 to say, in effect, "So when you are disciplined, quit feeling sorry for yourself. Keep your chin up and keep going— 'walk off' [133] your sorrow, even though you may not feel like it, because if you quit walking this path you'll be on one with a dead end."

---

133. Here we have employed an athletic phrase— "Walk it off!"— that is really quite pertinent. Many minor athletic injuries will heal as the person continues to use his injured part despite some pain, rather than give in to the natural tendency to quit playing and sit on the bench. The key in such cases is the mental aggressiveness of the athlete to compete and win (I Corinthians 9:24-27).

Hebrews 12:12,13

Therefore, strengthen your feeble arms and weak knees.

Make level paths for your feet, so that the lame may not be disabled, but rather healed.

We can think of three means by which God actively "chastens" His children. First, by way of His written Word. As each of us looks into it regularly and carefully, we will be reminded of how God wants us to live. If we are not living this way, the Word chastens us. Second, God can, of course, also reprove or correct His children by direct revelation, and He is more likely to get through to us when our hearts are attuned to Him.

The third way He can discipline us is via other Christians in the Body of Christ, and this is most likely to happen as we are knitting our hearts together with them. To do so requires regular, sustained fellowship based upon the truth of God's Word. This manner of intra-Church chastening can be either verbal (as in Galatians 2) or non-verbal, as when you are with another Christian and see him handle a situation in a very godly way and it reminds you of how you did not handle a similar situation.

Perhaps the most common way that people come to recognize the value of obedience to God is by suffering the consequences of their own disobedience. Of course this is not God actively "chastening" us at all. Sin has consequences— mentally, physically and spiritually. Yet some people harden their hearts to sin and ignore its horrible consequences. The Bible speaks of such men as those whose conscience is "seared as with a hot iron" (I Timothy 4:2). This has been going on for centuries. Over seven hundred years before Christ, Isaiah wrote about such people:

Isaiah 22:13

But see, there is joy and revelry, slaughtering of cattle and killing of sheep, eating of meat and drinking of wine! "Let us eat and drink," you say, "for tomorrow we die!"

Many other people, however, grow tired of their life of sin and decide they want something better than their self centered, dead-end existence. For those people, the Lord is waiting with open arms to welcome them into His heart and into the fellowship of believers.

Few Christians awake to find a personal memo from Jesus Christ telling them everything they are to do that day, and exactly how to do it. God expects us to learn by experience, as we walk with Him and the Lord Jesus Christ. Often a father will let his child struggle with, say, the assembly of a bicycle, so that he will learn the mechanics of it. The father does not, however, *hide some of the parts* in order to humble the child! God did give us intelligence and the capacity to learn, often by recognizing from unfavorable circumstances that we are not doing something right, and that we need to change.

Some of the choices we make may not be the best ones, and may even lead to some suffering. Could God announce from heaven in a loud trumpet voice every time someone was making a wrong decision? He could, but not without defeating His purpose of fellowship with free-will people. God expects us to think through what we do and count the cost of our actions (Luke 14:28). He also expects us to obey His written Word and learn from it, as well as from the mistakes and successes of others. Sadly, many Christians have not really taken this to heart. Far too many Christians expect "grace" to cover for all their mistakes or inexperience, and then somehow feel that God is to blame when things turn out badly for them.

It is part of His goodness and Fatherly kindness that He gives us the freedom to make decisions and learn from them. In this way we can learn the practicality of obedience to God. By practicing the presence of God and Christ in our lives and experientially learning to love and obey them, we will develop our own convictions about their love and goodness. These convictions will help us trust our heavenly Father and our Lord Jesus Christ, no matter what trials the Devil sends our way.

CHAPTER 13

TWO TEACHERS, TWO TESTS

How Does God Test Us?

Because of sin, we are constantly tested in this life. Many people say that God tests us with suffering to see if we will stay faithful to Him, but, as we have seen, such is not the case. Let us consider what a "test" is. We believe one valid definition is that a test is a challenge to measure your learning, growth and development. Some people say that experience is the best teacher. Why is this not true? Because experience gives the test question first and the answer later, if at all.

Think back to your favorite teacher in school. Would you say that he or she was teaching for the benefit of the students? Most likely. Does such a good teacher give tests? Absolutely. But a good teacher only gives a test *after* adequate instruction. Would a good teacher give a test that a student could not pass, or even get a perfect score on if had he mastered the material taught? No. What is the motive behind a good teacher's tests? Most assuredly it is the growth, maturing and learning of his students.

But what about a bad teacher, one jaded by countless muggings in the halls? Does he give tests? Oh yes, but they are unannounced tests covering material he has never taught, and they must be taken while having wisdom teeth removed without an anesthetic. What is his motive? Obviously it is to do damage to the students. You might even say it is to "steal, kill and destroy" (John 10:10a).

So it is in the spiritual battle: both the One True God, the Father of Jesus Christ, and the false god of this age, Satan, test us. [134] The difference is in their motives and in the types of tests they give. Satan tests us by tempting us to disobey God's Word— to our detriment. One place we can see this is in his temptations of Jesus in the wilderness (Luke 4:1ff; Matthew 4:1ff). But Jesus Christ overcame these temptations as well as all the others Satan threw at Him, and that is why He can now help us do likewise. How do we do so? By willingly taking the tests that God gives us. How does God test us? Simply by asking us to trust Him and "wholeheartedly obey the form of teaching to which we were entrusted" (Romans 6:17).

Only God's Word enables us to understand these things, and in it we will see that it is only by taking the tests God gives that we can successfully handle Satan's tests. That is, it is by trusting and obeying God that you can minimize the effects of the sin of Lucifer and Adam in your own life. Even in the Old Testament it was clear that God's instructions were for the benefit of His people, as the following verses attest.

---

134. It should be noted that in Scripture the same Greek word *peirazo* is translated "tempt," as well as "test," "try," "examine" or "prove." It is the context that determines how *peirazo* should be translated. A "temptation" is generally associated with an evil motive, while "prove" or "examine" are generally associated with a good motive, i.e., the success of the one being examined. Thus it is easy to tell that when the Bible says that Jesus was in the wilderness fasting for forty days and Satan came to "tempt" (*peirazo*) him, "tempt" is a good translation, because Satan wanted Christ to fail. This helps us understand why Scripture can say that God never tempts anyone (James 1:13). When Paul penned "Examine [*peirazo*] yourselves to see whether you are in the faith" (II Corinthians 13:5), he did not mean to "tempt" yourself, but rather to prove yourself, to try yourself. R.C.H. Lenski writes of this in his commentary: "The Corinthians are to apply the right tests to themselves as to 'whether they are in the faith.' To try and test oneself is simple enough. A few honest questions honestly answered soon reveal where one stands." (*The Interpretation of St. Paul's First and Second Epistles to the Corinthians*, by R.C.H. Lenski, Augsburg Pub. House, Minneapolis MN, 1963, page 1332.).

Deuteronomy 10:12,13

And now, O Israel, what does the Lord your God ask of you but to fear the Lord your God, to walk in all his ways, to love him, to serve the Lord your God with all your heart and with all your soul,

And to observe the Lord's commands and decrees that I am giving you today for your own good?

Some other simple biblical examples come to mind, such as the dietary and sanitary instructions in the Old Testament (cp. Leviticus 11,17; Deuteronomy 14), and the record where God told people to build a fence around the perimeter of their flat roofs so they wouldn't fall off (Deuteronomy 22:8).

As we stated earlier, God tests us by asking us to trust Him and do what He says. One of His goals is to build character in us. As a good "teacher," neither God nor the Lord Jesus will ever ask you to do something you cannot do, right? If you answered affirmatively, a great truth should dawn on you: *whenever* God tells you to do *anything*, you immediately know one thing: YOU CAN!!! Therefore, *you do*, especially since you know it is in your own best interests to be obedient to your heavenly Father.

Once upon a time, after we had innocently looked into resolving some apparent biblical contradictions, we suddenly found ourselves hanging on the face of a cliff as sheer as any logic we had ever heard of. Actually it wasn't that suddenly. We had volunteered for a rock-climbing school, been given adequate instruction and taken out to meet our granite fate.

"Climb *this?*" Well, maybe if we follow the instructions we were given, we can. Anyway, we eventually stood on top of the cliff, and guess what? Instead of lamenting how hard it had been to get there, we rejoiced in our accomplishment, looked over at an even higher rock and said, "We can climb that one." What is the principle? *Obstacles are opportunities for growth!* Let us now cite one of many Old Testament records of God's people facing an apparently insurmountable obstacle and God testing them to help them overcome it and grow in faith. You can read the biblical account in Joshua 3:1-17 and see if it matches our version, which follows.

Moses had died, and Joshua was leading Israel to the Promised Land. Closer and closer they got, and then— there it was! Just across the *flooded Jordan River!* Oh, no! In the face of this apparently insurmountable obstacle, what were God's instructions? He told Joshua to tell the priests carrying the ark of the covenant to go first, and for the people to follow at a distance. God said that the priests were to walk right into the flooded river and that when the soles of their feet touched the water, the river would divide so that all the people could cross into the Promised Land.

Does that sound like a test to you? Suppose you had been one of those priests? Do you think your heart would have been pounding as you neared the edge of the Jordan? Of course, they could have just put down the ark and said, "Hey, this is ridiculous, let's just live on this side of the river and enjoy the view of the Promised Land across the water."

Had they done so, two things would *not* have occurred. First, they would not have received from God what He wanted to give them to bless them— the Promised Land. Second, they would not have experienced what we believe was a substantial increase in their faith.

What do you think happened in their hearts when their feet touched that water and the river backed up fifteen miles?! Verse ten of Joshua Chapter Three tells us that it was this incident that would later give them courage to overcome greater obstacles in the future, i.e., the obstreperous "ites." [135] Obstacles are opportunities for growth, but *only* when we look to God for the solution, and act accordingly.

Jesus Christ, The Master Teacher

In the New Testament, when Jesus was teaching His disciples, He followed in the footsteps of His Heavenly Father. Take a look at the record of the first company picnic in the Bible.

John 6:3-6 (KJV)

And Jesus went up into a mountain, and there he sat with his disciples.

And the passover, a feast of the Jews, was nigh.

---

135. Canaanites, Hittites, Jebusites, Amorites, Perrizites (and Termites).

When Jesus then lifted up *his* eyes, and saw a great company come unto him, he saith unto Philip, Whence shall we buy bread, that these may eat?

And this he said to prove [*peirazo*=test] [136] him: for he himself knew what he would do.

Would a good teacher give a test with no previous instruction? No. By then Philip had been with Jesus for some time, and Jesus had been instructing him, as well as the other disciples, about how to trust God, even when the situation looked hopeless. We believe Philip could have passed the test with flying colors by doing the same miracle Jesus ended up doing, or at least recognizing that Jesus could have done it, but instead, he flunked.

John 6:7-9 (KJV)

Philip answered him, Two hundred pennyworth of bread is not sufficient for them, that every one of them may take a little.

One of his disciples, Andrew, Simon Peter's brother, saith unto him,

There is a lad here, which hath five barley loaves, and two small fishes: but what are they among so many?

Philip looked only at the natural resources that were available, and failed to look to God's supernatural resources as Jesus then did. Verses eight and nine are a riot. Andrew saw his classmate Philip failing the exam, and leaned in to help him: "Hey, there's a kid over here with five— oh, forget it, that won't help. I don't know the answer either." Jesus said, "You both flunk," and then proceeded to "correct their tests" by showing them what they could have done had they learned their lesson better. The same Lord will work with us today, teaching us and helping us to mature in faith and understanding. But we must "come to school" on a daily basis. We cannot be "truant" Christians and expect to learn and grow in grace.

You Can Test Yourself

How do you prove God's Word to yourself? By testing it (acting upon it) to see if it works. Remember, God could not have proven

---

136. See footnote #134.

Himself to Israel at the Jordan River had not the priests tried (tested) the Word He spoke to them.

Romans 12:2

Do not conform any longer to the pattern of this world, but be transformed by the renewing of your mind. Then you will be able to test and approve what God's will is— his good, pleasing and perfect will.

In the above verse, the phrase "test and approve" is translated from the Greek word *dokimazo*. [137] The Word of God instructs each Christian to test himself against the standards God has set and not against other men.

Galatians 6:4

Each one should test [*dokimazo*] his own actions. Then he can take pride in himself, without comparing himself to somebody else, for each one should carry his own load.

Each individual Christian can experience satisfying and joyous growth in faith as he tests God's Word for himself.

I Thessalonians 2:4

On the contrary, we speak as men approved [*dokimazo*] by God to be entrusted with the gospel. We are not trying to please men but God, who tests [*dokimazo*] our hearts.

---

137. The following excerpts (part of a comparison of *dokimazo* and *peirazo*) are taken from *Wuest's Word Studies from the Greek New Testament*, Volume II— "Treasures" (Wm. B. Eerdman's Pub. Co., Grand Rapids MI, 1941) pages 126-131. [*Dokimazo*] refers to the act of testing someone or something for the purpose of approving it...The word has in it the idea of proving a thing whether it be worthy to be received or not...[It] implies that the trial itself was made in the expectation and hope that the issue would be such...The other word is *peirazo*. The word first meant "to pierce, search, attempt." Then it came to mean "to try or test intentionally, and with the purpose of discovering what good or evil, what power or weakness, was in a person or thing." But the fact that men so often break down under this test gave *peirazo* a predominant sense of putting to the proof with the intention and the hope that the one put to the test may break down under the test. Thus the word is used constantly of the solicitations and suggestions of Satan. *Dokimazo* is used generally of God, but never of Satan, for Satan never puts to the test in order that he may approve. *Peirazo* is used at times of God, but only in the sense of testing in order to discover what evil or good may be in a person.

How does God test our hearts? By entrusting us with the Gospel, which He tells us to act upon.

II Corinthians 13:5a

Examine [*peirazo*] yourselves to see whether you are in the faith; test [*dokimazo*] yourselves.

In the above verse, the word "examine" is not *dokimazo*, but *peirazo*, which means to attempt or to endeavor, as well as to try or to test. It is usually translated "tempt," as in the gospel accounts of Jesus' temptation (see Matthew 4:1,3; Luke 4:2) but it is also used of God's proving men (Hebrews 11:17). It comes from the root word meaning "to pierce," and briefly elaborating upon it at this point may serve to make its definition clearer.

When you want to find out whether or not a cake you are baking is done, you pierce it, usually with a toothpick (or a tire iron, depending upon your culinary experience). Meanwhile, back at the grill, the one cooking the steak does likewise. Why? Because both cooks want to know what's on the inside, (or, you might say, what it's made of) so they examine the object by piercing it.

When the Devil tempted Jesus, he "stuck" Him the first time and said, "Hungry? Why not make some stone-bread?" But when the Devil pulled out his blade, there was a note on it that said, "It is written." Each time the Devil "pierced" Jesus with temptation, He responded with "It is written." You might say Jesus "bled Bible." Why? Because He was the *Living Word*, Who always obeyed His Father, no matter what the Devil's tests. Finally the Devil said, "Heck, this guy'll never be done."

If we are convinced that God is on our side and that obstacles are opportunities for growth, we are inspired to face them with a sense of joyous determination, and persevere until they are behind us. Because we have "Christ" in us (Colossians 1:27) via holy spirit, we need not fear being pierced, because then we will see what we are made of.

James 1:2-4

Consider it pure joy, my brothers, whenever you face trials of many kinds,

Because you know that the testing of your faith develops perseverance.

Perseverance must finish its work so that you may be mature and complete, not lacking anything.

See the point? It is not the trial itself that is the cause of joy, but knowing that the testing of your faith results in endurance. Then you can "count it all joy," that is, relish the challenge as an opportunity to see God work in your life and reveal Himself to you in new ways.

"Counting it all joy" is a great key to victorious living. Jesus Christ was the quintessential example of one who did this in the face of great adversity—the torture and pain of the cross. "For the joy that was set before him," Jesus endured the cross for us (Hebrews 12:2). Many of the trials and tribulations in our lives pale in comparison to those of our Lord's, and yet we too can endure in the midst of affliction. How?

Hebrews 12:3

Consider him who endured such opposition from sinful men, so that you will not grow weary and lose heart.

The example Christ gave us of walking with our Heavenly Father, that of totally entrusting Himself to His heavenly Father and obeying Him every step of the way, is, for us, a pattern to copy. As He endured and overcame with the help of God, so can we, if we walk in His steps, that is, entrust ourselves entirely to God. Amen!

CHAPTER 14

GOD'S INFINITE RESOURCEFULNESS

Turning Lemons Into Lemonade

As we have stated, our faith facilitates God's power changing a situation. No matter how bleak a situation may appear, we must remember that with God, nothing is impossible. As has often been said, God is very good at "making lemonade out of lemons." He says just about exactly that in Romans 8:28, a tremendous verse of Scripture. Unfortunately this verse is so poorly translated in *The King James Version* (and in some others) that those aforementioned "countless Christians" have used it to say that all tragedy, sickness and death is "good" for God's people and is a part of His plan for them.

Romans 8:28 (KJV)

And we know that all things work together for good to them that love God, to them who are the called according to His purpose.

This inaccurate translation has contributed to the erroneous belief held by countless Christians that the pain and suffering in their lives is God's will and is somehow for their own good. But, as Richard Rice states:

> According to the Bible, suffering is a consequence of sin. It was not a part of God's original design for this world at all. So the view that suffering is anything other than evil is incorrect. It is inherently opposed to the will of God. And since our lives contain evil as well as good, it is evident that the view that God plans everything that happens to us is false...The tragedies of life are real. The grace of God can mitigate the consequences of evil and bring out spiritual good, but it does not necessarily restore things to exactly their former condition. No matter how much good results, evil is never "more than made up for," in a temporal sense. It often involves, to a greater or lesser degree, permanent loss. So whatever the spiritual or material good that follows the negative experiences of life, it is due entirely to the providential activity of God, not to something positive or beneficial in the experiences themselves. [138]

No doubt some people, even though they believed that God was responsible for their affliction, have, because of their mental resolve, come through much suffering better off for it. This is so often the case that we, the authors, feel that it is a major reason why the teaching that God either causes or allows suffering continues in Christian circles. The fact is, however, that there are many people who have *not* endured suffering with their faith intact. How many people, thinking that a supreme, omnipotent God was causing them or someone they love indescribable anguish, have turned away from Him? How much easier it is to endure trials when you have the absolute confidence that they are not caused by God and that He is working as hard as He can in your behalf, as Romans 8:28 says. The *New International Version* translates this verse much better than does the *King James Version*.

Romans 8:28

And we know that IN ALL THINGS God works for the good of those who love him, who have been called according to his purpose.

---

138. Rice, *When Bad Things Happen To God's People*, pages 40, 41, 45, 46.

It is important to see the difference between these translations of Romans 8:28. People that hold to the *King James Version* say that "all things work together for good...." In other words, losing your job, getting cancer, or the death of someone close to you is somehow good. The NIV translation (which we feel much more accurately reflects the Greek text) says that God is working for your good in every situation. Maybe you have lost your job, have cancer, or have had someone close to you die. These things are not good, but God is working for your good in these situations. Knowing this helps you cleave to Him and allows Him to help you. On the other hand, *blaming* Him automatically negates your trust in Him for help. Richard Rice very articulately elaborates on God's prowess in working with the "lemons" of life:

> God works through secondary causes to achieve His objectives. And it reaches its highest expression in God's use of developments that are inherently opposed to His will to accomplish His purposes. To respond creatively to suffering, we need to appreciate God's ability to incorporate the negative experiences of life into the fulfillment of His plans for us.

> We often speak of "God's plan for our lives." But just what this expression means is not at all clear in the thinking of many people. What picture do you get when you think of God's plan for your life? Is God's plan for you like a writer's script for a play— all written out, with every scene carefully plotted in advance? Has God arranged everything that will ever happen to you, down to the last detail? Does every experience have an assigned place in your life?

> Many people are convinced that this is the case. In their view, confidence in divine sovereignty requires us to believe that God is somehow responsible for all that happens to us and that everything we experience is for the best. Indeed, nothing just "happens." God plans it all...

> Another way of thinking about God's relation to our lives makes more theological sense, and it is more helpful on a personal level too. According to this view, God is intimately involved in our lives, not by working out a plan that is fixed in every detail, but by responding creatively to everything that happens. God has certain basic objectives for us, but in

order to reach them, He interacts with events and decisions [in our lives], for which He is not responsible.

Pain and suffering do not come to us because God planned it that way. There is nothing inherently good about these experiences. But once they are here, God can bring good out of them and use them to accomplish something positive. [139]

How about a classic biblical example? Okay— Joseph (Genesis 37-50). Was it God's will that he was hated by his brothers, sold into slavery, framed by Potiphar's wife and thrown into jail? No. Was God responsible for these evils? No. But, because Joseph stayed faithful to look to Him and to trust Him, God was able to work mightily in the whole situation, not only to enable Joseph to endure, but to the glorious end of his personal deliverance and exaltation, and Israel's salvation also. When Joseph had become the Pharaoh's righthand man, and his brothers stood before him, he said to them, "You plotted evil against me, but God turned it into good, in order to preserve the lives of many people" (Genesis 50:20— *Good News Bible*). [140] Now *that's* lemonade!

In the early days of television in the USA, a children's show featured an artist whose creativity was astounding, and illustrative of God's resourcefulness. This artist would sit beside an easel with a large pad of white paper. Randomly he would hand a piece of charcoal to one of the children and have him make any sort of scribble he wanted. He would then ask the children what they would like him to make out of the scribble. It might be an animal, a clown, or anything that appealed to the children's imagination or seemed to pose a big challenge to the artist's skill. The artist then went to work transforming the scribble into the requested image with amazing ease and skill. It didn't seem to matter what the scribble looked like or what he was asked to make out of it— he could do it.

We must see God in a similar light, and appreciate His creative genius. He can take any set of circumstances and, with a few master

---

139. *Ibid.*, page 40, 41.

140. We believe this translation more clearly represents what actually happened than does the KJV: "God meant it for good," or the NIV: "God intended it." In His creative resourcefulness, God gave this incident His own meaning, and used it to achieve His purposes. Joseph was a type of Christ, and the same principle is illustrated in Acts 2:22, 23, where we see that God gave His own meaning to Christ's death.

strokes of grace and mercy, bring a new picture into view, one that shows His love and will. There is nothing that Satan and sin can introduce into our lives that God cannot transform into something that will glorify Him. There is one important difference between the artist and God, however. The artist took the charcoal from the child and drew the picture himself. God works *with us* to guide us as we and He draw the picture together. He asks us to work together with Him to achieve His will— by praying, trusting Him, obeying Him, and speaking His Word. As the English proverb well expresses it: "God supplies the milk, we bring the pail."

Richard Rice points out that such thinking may seem to some as though it compromises God's "sovereignty," and leaves Him at the mercy of what people do. He then gives two ways to answer this objection.

In the first place, God has voluntarily limited His sovereignty over the world in order to leave us free to choose. When He created morally free beings, He, in effect, shared with them the power to determine what course history would take. So whatever limits there are to God's power, they are limits which He voluntarily set when He decided to create the kind of world He made.

In the second place, the ability to respond creatively to events as they happen, so that they contribute to His purposes, takes, if anything, a higher kind of power than the ability to plan to the last detail everything that happens. [141]

Turning Tragedy Into Triumph

God's limitless resourcefulness allows Him to attach His own meaning to many negative events. No doubt the best example of this is the most negative event of all time— the death of His Son Jesus Christ. Acts 2:23 says that the Jews, chiefly their rulers, "by wicked hands" crucified and slew Jesus. This is also the testimony of the gospel records (Matthew 27:1,2; Mark 15:1; etc.). Though the Jewish religious leaders were the instigators, the Roman government carried out the crucifixion, and would have broken His legs to kill Him,

141. Rice, *When Bad Things Happen to God's People*, page 41.

but Scripture says He was dead already (Matthew 27:50), having "given up the ghost."

In I Corinthians 2:8, however, "the princes of this world" (i.e., Satan and his hosts) are blamed for crucifying Jesus. Had they known about the power of Jesus' resurrection and the subsequent outpouring of the gift of holy spirit on Pentecost, they would have let Him live. So we see that it was actually Satan, behind the scenes "pulling the strings," who was responsible for Jesus' death.

Philippians 2:5 reveals that Jesus obeyed God unto death and crucifixion, indicating that this was God's will for Him so that He might redeem man. Acts 2:23 says that He was delivered by the determinate counsel and foreknowledge of God, who knew that His Son would have to be sacrificed and killed. God knew that by having His Son die for sin and sinners, He would be able to rectify the sin problem for all time. God did not, however, work in evil men to have them do what He wanted them to do, for then He would be unrighteous and manipulative. But, as with Joseph, what the Devil and wicked men freely chose to do and meant for evil, God turned into something that ultimately contributed to His purposes for mankind.

Our wonderful God's superior wisdom and power enable Him to bring about a redemptive meaning out of even the darkest of circumstances, as in the death of His only begotten Son. How He is able to allow created beings total freedom to oppose Him, yet still bring to pass His overall will is marvelous beyond our comprehension, and is why we love and worship Him as we do.

The following story further illustrates how God can resourcefully incorporate unplanned, negative developments in our lives into the fulfillment of His purposes for us. It also points to Jesus Christ as the supreme example of redemptive suffering:

> John Ruskin was once in the company of a lady who dropped a blot of ink on her beautiful silk handkerchief. "Oh," she cried in great dismay, "my lovely handkerchief is ruined." "Perhaps not," said Ruskin, "please leave it with me."

> A little later he returned her handkerchief, but it was no longer disfigured. Unable to remove the blot, Ruskin had used it as a basis for a most attractive design. The handkerchief, far from being ruined, was now even lovelier than it had been.

It is the making possible of a transformation of this nature that is the Gospel's answer to the problem of suffering, a transformation of even the most unsightly blots that may happen along to disfigure our lives. This is what Jesus did with the suffering that came His own way. He accepted it without bitterness or rancor and transformed it.

This is supremely illustrated in the Cross. No greater tragedy could be imagined than this, no fate more undeserved, no suffering more agonizing. Yet out of it Jesus brought good. He took all the suffering and evil that was Calvary and out of it He fashioned the greatest victory that history has ever seen— and the most important. [142]

Rice states:

God's capacity to work for good in the world extends to everything that happens. Nothing lies beyond His ability to respond to things creatively and work toward the fulfillment of His purposes. In many ways, the Bible is one long record of God's response to the mistakes and failures of human beings, and of His ability to bring something good from even the most negative experiences. [143]

It is ironic that God is so adept at turning tragedy into triumph that often people mistakenly attribute to Him not only the solution, but also the problem. Rice says basically the same thing: "We must be careful not to view the benefits that follow something negative as evidence that God intended it to happen to begin with." [144] Understanding how God's awesome love, wisdom and power can turn even the most negative situation into a positive one greatly encourages us to steadfastly look to Him in faith and hope.

Once more Richard Rice waxes eloquent:

This means that for someone who is open to God's creative, redemptive power, nothing is totally negative. It means that in a life committed to God there are no wasted years. A Christian can look back, over the entire course of his life, and thank God for His guidance in everything that happened—

---

142. Martin, *Suffering Man/Loving God*, pages 68-69.

143. Rice, *When Bad Things Happen to God's People*, page 23.

144. *Ibid.*, page 45.

the bad as well as the good. And this transforms life's negative experiences and apparent defeats. It means that nothing is a total loss...God's ability to work for good applies not only to things that happen to us, but also to things we bring on ourselves. Even when our problems result from a lack of judgment or from outright rebellion, God can bring about something good, if we repent and patiently trust Him to work things out. Nothing lies totally beyond the reach of His transforming and creative power. In all things, He works for good. [145]

Having this confidence in God's goodness and creative ability, we are now in a position to understand how suffering can have value in one's life, without having to attribute it to God.

---

145. *Ibid.*, page 45.

CHAPTER 15

THE REDEMPTIVE VALUE OF SUFFERING

Count It All Joy

God's love, His wisdom and His amazing resourcefulness give us a firm foundation for faith in His promises even amidst the trials and tribulations of life. In this chapter, we will address how a Christian's proper response to evil and suffering can result in spiritual growth in his life. Understanding that God is not responsible for suffering, and that He and Jesus Christ want to deliver us from it, is fundamental to our responding to it with the right attitude. But there is more we can learn to help us do so.

At this point, let us briefly discuss the word "suffering," and again define it as it is used in this book. Dictionary definitions use words like "loss," "distress," affliction," "pain," etc. In the *King James Version*, more than a dozen Greek words are translated as "suffer," "suffering," etc., and these Greek words contain a wide range of meaning. Remember our simple definition in the Introduction—mental or physical pain or anguish. It is sad to say, but almost everyone knows what suffering is.

Many people will no doubt think of suffering in terms of deprivation of material things, but what to one person is being "deprived" is not so to another. With the goal of further clarifying what suffering is, from God's perspective, we should briefly point out the biblical ideal in terms of material things. It is not suffering to have to drive a Yugo rather than a Mercedes.

I Timothy 6:6-8

But godliness with contentment is great gain.

For we brought nothing into the world, and we can take nothing out of it.

But if we have food and clothing, we will be content with that.

Perhaps more than anything else that comes our way in life, suffering tests our faith. Suffering can either make or break a person, depending upon his understanding of, and faith in, the Word of God. If one mistakenly attributes the source of his suffering to *God*, he may very well take the attitude that Job's wife recommended to him: "Curse God and die" (Job 2:9). "Thank you, dear."

Suffering can also have the opposite effect—it can be a catalyst for beneficial growth in faith for those who persevere in trusting the Lord. After all, it is pressure that turns coal into diamonds. And remember the old sayings that the same sun that melts the wax hardens the clay, and the same hammer that shatters the glass forges the steel. Thus we can, and should, approach whatever "life" throws at us with the aggressive attitude set forth in the following verses, which we have already mentioned:

James 1:2,3

Consider it pure joy, my brothers, whenever you face trials of many kinds,

Because you know that the testing of your faith develops perseverance.

A Piece Of The Action

At this point, a clear distinction needs to be made between suffering that arises simply from having to live in a fallen world, and the suffering a Christian experiences when he gets into the spiritual battle and "steps into harm's way." Because the Devil is the god of this age, and insanely wicked, he does his best to see to it that every person suffers some sickness, hardships, etc. God and Jesus Christ need people who will volunteer to be "fellow workers" (I Corinthians 3:9), "ambassadors" (II Corinthians 5:20) and "good soldiers" (II Timothy 2:3) for them. Christians who serve Christ in this manner will often suffer persecution in ways that Christians who "lie low" will not, as the following verse makes plain:

II Timothy 3:12

In fact, everyone who wants to live a godly life in Christ Jesus will be persecuted.

Let us allow the Apostle Paul, one who certainly understood what suffering was all about, to elaborate:

Philippians 1:27-30

Whatever happens, conduct yourselves in a manner worthy of the gospel of Christ. Then, whether I come and see you or only hear about you in my absence, I will know that you stand firm in one spirit, contending as one man for the faith of the gospel

Without being frightened in any way by those who oppose you. This is a sign to them that they will be destroyed, but that you will be saved— and that by God.

For it has been granted to you on behalf of Christ not only to believe on him, but also to suffer [146] for him,

Since you are going through the same struggle you saw I had, and now hear that I still have.

---

146. The Greek noun most often translated "suffering" is *pathema*, and means "evil suffered; affliction" (Bullinger *Lexicon*, p. 749). "The verb *pascho* means 'to experience' or 'to undergo' in either a good or bad sense. Yet its usage developed in such a way that *pascho* came to be used less and less frequently in a good sense, and never that way without some clear indication, at least from the context, when the good sense was meant." (Bauer *Lexicon*, p. 633). In the New Testament, it is used exclusively of suffering evil, never of experiencing good.

God's Word exhorts the Christian to hate evil (Romans 12:9). This hatred is very healthy, as long as it does not supersede our love for God as our primary motivation to serve Him. When it comes to the spiritual battle, each Christian needs a "killer instinct." When you get knocked down, rather than staying down and giving up on God or yourself, get up swinging!

When we, the Church, stand fast on God's Word and fearlessly work together for the Lord in the face of adversarial opposition, it makes the greatness of our salvation more real to us, and reminds Satan and his hordes of their impending doom (Ephesians 3:10). Philippians 1:29 is eye-opening for many Christians who have been taught that Christianity is, in this life, supposed to be a piece of cake, a bowl of cherries, like taking candy from a baby or some other tasty analogy.

But don't worry about going hungry. We have the Bread of Life, the milk and the meat of the Word and rivers of living water. As we faithfully partake of ("drink in," "eat up," "digest") the life and teachings of our Lord, our identification with Him becomes more complete, not only doctrinally, but also in practice, that is, in living day by day.

Romans Chapter Six tells us that when we were born again, we became spiritually identified with Jesus Christ in His death, His burial, His resurrection and His walk in newness of life. Ephesians Chapter Two tells us that we can also identify with being ascended and seated with Him. Philippians talks about the practical side of these doctrinal truths, and in the context of its corrective emphasis, the implication is that the Philippian church still had too much pride in its earthly accomplishments. The following verses are a clarion call to each Christian to assess his own priorities:

Philippians 3:7-10

But whatever was to my profit [his previous religious credentials listed in verses 5-6] I now consider loss for the sake of Christ.

What is more, I consider everything a loss compared to the surpassing greatness of knowing Christ Jesus my Lord, for whose sake I have lost all things. I consider them rubbish, that I may gain Christ

And be found in him, not having a righteousness of my own that comes from the law, but that which is through faith in Christ— the righteousness that comes from God and is by faith.

I want to know [experientially] Christ and the power of his resurrection and the fellowship of his sufferings, becoming like him in his death, and so, somehow, to attain to the resurrection from the dead.

Paul's attitude is, for each Christian, well worth emulating. He so appreciated his Lord's sacrifice for him that he too wanted "a piece of the action," so to speak. Perhaps, while writing to the Philippians, Paul recalled the courageous example of Peter and the other apostles who some years earlier had stood before the Sanhedrin, of which Paul had most likely been a member prior to his conversion. [147] After they had been beaten and ordered not to speak in the name of Jesus:

Acts 5:41,42

The apostles left the Sanhedrin, rejoicing because they had been counted worthy of suffering disgrace for the Name.

Day after day, in the temple courts and from house to house, they never stopped teaching and proclaiming the good news that Jesus is the Christ.

Paul was a competitor who knew that Jesus had equipped him for the fight, and he enthusiastically desired to lay his life on the line for the One who had died for him. A great part of his motivation was his understanding and assurance of the rewards that awaited him in Paradise, rewards similar to those that will be given to every believer who stands for the One True God.

Suffering And Glory

The apostle Peter had the same competitive attitude as did Paul, though Peter had once rebelled against the thought of Christ having to suffer (Matthew 16:21-23). It is interesting that of the 42 occur-

---

147. V.J. Conybeare and J.S. Howson, *The Life and Epistles of St. Paul*, (Wm. B. Eerdmans Pub. Co., Grand Rapids MI, Fifteenth reprinting, April 1978), page 64.

rences of the verb "to suffer" (*pascho*), 12 of them are in Peter's first epistle. In the second chapter, he cites the classic example of the proper attitude to have in the face of suffering, especially that inflicted by other people, which is often the most difficult to bear.

I Peter 2:20-23

But how is it to your credit if you receive a beating for doing wrong and endure it? But if you suffer for doing good and you endure it, this is commendable before God.

To this you were called, because Christ suffered for you, leaving you an example, that you should follow in his steps.

He committed no sin, and no deceit was found in his mouth.

When they hurled their insults at him, he did not retaliate; when he suffered, he made no threats. Instead, he entrusted himself to him who judges justly.

Jesus Christ *entrusted Himself to God*, His Father. We can walk in His steps and do likewise, manifesting His gentleness and His courage.

I Peter 3:14-17

But even if you should suffer for what is right, you are blessed. Do not fear what they fear; do not be frightened.

But in your hearts set apart Christ as Lord. Always be prepared to give an answer to everyone who asks you to give the reason for the hope that you have. But do this with gentleness and respect,

Keeping a clear conscience, so that those who speak maliciously against your good behavior in Christ may be ashamed of their slander.

It is better, if it is God's will, to suffer for doing good than for doing evil.

Part of what it means to "set apart Christ as Lord" is to be willing to suffer for His sake. In verse 17 we see the phrase "if it is God's will." One might jump on this phrase and ride it off, far from the total context of Scripture, proclaiming thereby that it is sometimes God's will that Christians suffer. But that is not what the verse is saying, for if so it would contradict many other sections of God's Word. What the verse is emphasizing is that it is better to suffer for speaking the Word than for, say, car theft. It is not God's will that we suffer, but it *is* His will that we "do good," even if it leads to our suffering.

We must understand not only that we are living in a war zone, but also that we are *targets*, and that we may suffer for doing God's will. When we realize this, we are not bewildered when tribulation comes our way, mistakenly thinking that it is either God's fault or our own, and we do not shrink from it (Galatians 6:12).

I Peter 4:12-16

Dear friends, do not be surprised at the painful trial you are suffering, as though something strange were happening to you.

But rejoice that you participate in the sufferings of Christ, so that you may be overjoyed when his glory is revealed.

If you are insulted because of the name of Christ, you are blessed, for the Spirit of glory and of God rests on you.

If you suffer, it should not be as a murderer or thief or any other kind of criminal, or even as a meddler.

However, if you suffer as a Christian, do not be ashamed, but praise God that you bear that name.

In verse 12, the word "suffering" is from *peirazo*, meaning to test or to try. The Devil tested Jesus, remember? He pierced Him over and over. What do you think he'll try to do to you, a part of the Body of Christ? Look at the attitude we are to have when "pierce-secution" comes. A key to rejoicing amid suffering is anticipating the glory that will follow. In I Peter 4:13 (above), and in other verses, the word "glory" relates at least in part to the *rewards* we will receive when our Lord appears.

I Peter 5:1

To the elders among you, I appeal as a fellow elder, a witness of Christ's sufferings and one who also will share in the glory to be revealed:

Here again we see the correlation between suffering and glory. We think that Peter not only meant that he had personally seen Jesus suffer, but also that he had "earned his own stripes" by standing boldly for the Lord.

I Peter 5:8-11

Be self-controlled and alert. Your enemy the devil prowls around like a roaring lion looking for someone to devour.

Resist him, standing firm in the faith, because you know that your brothers throughout the world are undergoing the same kind of sufferings.

And the God of all grace, who called you to his eternal glory in Christ, after you have suffered a little while, will himself restore you and make you strong, firm and steadfast.

To him be the power for ever and ever. Amen.

At this point let us deal with the question, "What if standing for the truth costs me my life?" Countless believers in the One True God have faced that question, and many have died proclaiming their faith. Well, based upon a godly, long-term-gain perspective that includes our future rewards, there are worse things than dying for the Lord—such as turning our backs on the One who died for us. The fact that Jesus conquered death assures us that if we die before He appears, we simply sleep until He awakens us to everlasting life. [148] In that light, while it is still an enemy to be despised and avoided by any means short of compromising God's Word, death loses its fearsome hold on us.

The Old Testament believers Shadrach, Meshach and Abednego have provided us with a sterling example of commitment and courage (Daniel 3). When told that they would be thrown into the fiery furnace if they did not bow before the king's idol when the band played,

Daniel 3:16-18

Shadrach, Meshach and Abednego replied to the king, "O Nebuchadnezzar, we do not need to defend ourselves before you in this matter.

If we are thrown into the blazing furnace, the God we serve is able to save us from it, and he will rescue us from your hand, O king.

---

148. Graeser, Lynn, Schoenheit, *Is There Death After Life?* (available from CES).

But even if he does not, we want you to know, O king, that we will not serve your gods or worship the image of gold you have set up."

Awesome! This does not indicate a complacent attitude toward death, but rather a fearless one based upon a realization of resurrection. Fear of death is a definite distraction to faith in the delivering power of God, because, as the following verses show, such fear puts people in bondage.

Hebrews 2:14,15

Since the children have flesh and blood, he too shared in their humanity so that by his death he might destroy him who holds the power of death— that is, the devil—

And free those who all their lives were held in slavery by their fear of death.

Death is the Devil's best punch, but Jesus took it, got up off the canvas and is winding up to deliver His own final haymaker!

Our Proper Response To Suffering Helps Others

It is said that "no man is an island." For Christians, this is certainly true. Remember I Peter 5:9, which says that your brothers and sisters in the Lord are faced with the same sufferings you are? That is why we can help one another if we deal with Satan's tests in a godly manner. This fact should be added incentive for us to do so. The following verses aptly express this truth:

II Corinthians 1:3-7

Praise be to the God and Father of our Lord Jesus Christ, the Father of compassion and the God of all comfort,

Who comforts us in all our troubles, so that we can comfort those in any trouble with the comfort we ourselves have received from God.

For just as the sufferings of Christ flow over into our lives, so also through Christ our comfort overflows.

If we are distressed, it is for your comfort and salvation; if we are comforted, it is for your comfort, which produces in you patient endurance of the same sufferings we suffer.

And our hope for you is firm, because we know that just as you share in our sufferings, so also you share in our comfort.

Obstacles are opportunities for growth, remember? Verse five shows that the bigger the obstacle, the more comfort, strength and wisdom the Lord will give you to help you deal with it. Once you are on the other side of the challenge, you get to keep all that you learned and gained in the experience. Thus you have experienced "growth."

II Corinthians 1:5 (above) speaks of "the sufferings of Christ flowing over into our lives." This is one of several passages of Scripture that touch upon a Christian's identification with the sufferings of his Savior. Here are some others:

Colossians 1:24

Now I rejoice in what was suffered for you, and I fill up [complete] in my flesh what is still lacking in regard to Christ's afflictions, for the sake of his body, which is the church.

Philippians 3:10

I want to know Christ and the power of his resurrection and the fellowship of sharing in his sufferings, becoming like him in his death, and so, somehow, to attain to the resurrection from the dead.

Although we may not understand it all, "the fellowship of sharing in his sufferings" somehow enables us to be a part of Christ's redemptive ministry, and it benefits others, as did His suffering. If you look back to II Corinthians 1:3-7 (above), you can see this truth. Verse 5 says that though the sufferings of Christ flow over into our lives, "so also through Christ our comfort overflows." Why? Because, as Hebrews 4:15 states, we do not have a Lord "who is unable to sympathize with our weaknesses, but we have one who has been tempted in every way, just as we are— yet without sin."

When properly understood from Scripture, the magnitude of Jesus' sufferings— physical and emotional— far exceeds what most Christians will have to endure. Let us remember that He basically suffered *alone*, in terms of human companionship. He knows that companionship is vital for suffering people, and He will always be with us, no matter what our circumstances. "Because he himself suffered when he was tempted, he is able to help those who are being tempted" (Hebrews 2:18). That is why each of us should "approach the throne of grace with confidence, so that we may receive mercy and find grace to help us in our time of need" (Hebrews 4:16).

Certainly the Apostle Paul's ability to deal with all that he suffered (see II Corinthians 11:23ff) was in large part due to his comprehending the truths that he himself would later set forth in Scripture. Paul fully realized, even while alone in his sufferings, that how he responded would affect the lives of many other Christians. We too can be motivated to faithfulness by this same truth. No Christian is "the Lone Ranger." There is comfort and strength in standing shoulder-to-shoulder in battle and supporting one another in times of suffering, because your example of resolute faith and joy can encourage others, and vice versa. Here we are talking about what we like to call "the camaraderie of the committed," one of the true joys of life.

Furthermore, suffering can actually contribute to the hope of Paradise being magnified in our hearts. As Rice says:

> Suffering reminds us that something is drastically wrong with our present situation...One effect of sin is our tendency to find satisfaction in things of less than ultimate value. We are in constant danger of becoming so comfortable with the temporal material things that we lose sight of the eternal. Suffering jolts us into realizing that our destiny lies beyond this world. [149]

God promises us that He will strengthen us in time of trouble, and one day by His power and grace glorify Himself in us in the age to come. At the bottom line of life's balance sheet is our hope of everlasting life, guaranteed to each Christian by the gift of holy spirit.

Romans 5:1-5

> Therefore, since we have been justified through faith, we have peace with God through our Lord Jesus Christ,

---

149. Rice, *When Bad Things Happen to God's People*, page 59.

Through whom we have gained access by faith into this grace in which we now stand. And we rejoice in the hope of the glory of God.

Not only so, but we also rejoice in our sufferings, because we know that suffering produces perseverance;

Perseverance, character [*dokime*— what is produced by passing the test]; and character, hope.

And hope does not disappoint us, because God has poured out his love into our hearts by the Holy Spirit, whom [holy spirit which] he has given us.

CHAPTER 16

HIS STRENGTH IN OUR WEAKNESS

Called To A Holy Purpose

So here we are in a spiritual war zone "behind enemy lines" until the Lord Jesus shows up to rescue us from this present evil age. How do we approach the challenges we encounter in the Adversary's domain? With the supernatural power of God resident within us in the gift of His spirit.

II Timothy 1:7-12

For God did not give us a spirit of timidity, but a spirit of power, of love and of self-discipline.

So do not be ashamed to testify about our Lord, or ashamed of me his prisoner. But join with me in suffering for the gospel, by the power of God,

Who has saved us and called us to a holy life— not because of anything we have done but because of his own purpose and grace. This grace was given us in Christ Jesus before the beginning of time,

But it has now been revealed through the appearing of our Savior, Christ Jesus, who has destroyed death and has brought life and immortality to light through the gospel.

And of this gospel I was appointed a herald and an apostle and a teacher.

That is why I am suffering as I am. Yet I am not ashamed, because I know whom I have believed, and am convinced that he is able to guard what I have entrusted to him for that day.

Note in verse eight that it is by the power of God working in and with us that we can persevere despite suffering, knowing that we have been called by God to a holy purpose that will be consummated in the age to come. This brings us to a major point we want to emphasize as we near the end of this book. In its notes on II Corinthians 4:11, the *NIV Study Bible* puts it well by saying that "human weakness provides the occasion for the triumph of divine power." The sooner we recognize our own inability, the sooner we can, by association, remember and lean upon the Lord Jesus Christ's supernatural ability in us. This is a great key to looking at life's challenges with encouragement rather than discouragement.

II Corinthians 4:8,9

We are hardpressed on every side, but not crushed; perplexed, but not in despair;

Persecuted, but not abandoned; struck down, but not destroyed.

In verse eight, the word "perplexed" means "not knowing which way to go," while "in despair" means to think there *is* no way to go. But, as the verse says, we are *not* in despair, because the truth is that there *is* always a way to be faithful to God, Who never abandons us, and helps us find the way.

II Corinthians 4:10-12

We always carry around in our body the death of Jesus, so that the life of Jesus may also be revealed in our body.

For we who are alive are always being given over to death for Jesus' sake, so that his life may be revealed in our mortal body.

So then, death is at work in us, but life is at work in you.

The epistles to the Corinthians relate closely to the doctrine set forth in Romans, and the above three verses illustrate that. To magnify the power of Christ in us rather than magnifying our own weakness, we must consistently reckon the "old man" dead and "walk in newness of life" (Romans 6:11). This is what verses 10-12 (above) are all about. As the *NIV Study Bible* notes put it, "daily 'dying' magnifies the wonder of daily resurrection life."

A Thorny Issue

The apostle Paul endured a tremendous amount of persecutions and afflictions, so one special thing that God did to help him do so was to give him a technicolor vision of the future Paradise (II Corinthians 12:4). The Word of God teaches that the future hope is the anchor of our souls (Hebrews 6:19), i.e., the more firmly we have the hope of our wonderful future in mind, the less likely we are to drift away (or be pulled away) from God and the things of God. The Lord knew what Paul was enduring, and gave him the vision of Paradise to help him stay firmly resolved. [150] Just after Paul recounts some of the revelation he received, there is a section most pertinent to our subject, and one that has too often been misunderstood. Paul writes of a thorn in his flesh. [151]

---

150. God has helped many others in hard times by giving them visions and revelation. For example, God helped Jesus anticipate His suffering and death. In the vision God gave Jesus on the Mount of Transfiguration, the subject that Moses and Elijah talked with Him about was His death (Luke 9:31).

151. *Introduction To God's Heart*, Tape 8, Side B. Also *Christ The Healer*, F.F. Bosworth (Originally published 1877; Reprint by Fleming H. Revell Company, USA, 1973) "Paul's Thorn," page 190. Bosworth does a great job of showing from Scripture that Paul's "thorn in the flesh" was the people who were persecuting and afflicting him. Our point in this book is not to debate what the thorn was, but rather to recognize that the Bible teaches it was from Satan, not from God.

II Corinthians 12:7 (KJV)

And lest I should be exalted above measure through the abundance of the revelations, there was given to me a thorn in the flesh, the messenger of Satan to buffet me, lest I should be exalted above measure.

Most Christians attribute Paul's "thorn in the flesh" to *God*, but God says it was a messenger of *Satan*. The *New International Version* makes this verse sound like the "thorn" was given to Paul by God to keep him from becoming "conceited" about getting such an awesome revelation as "the Paradise movie." Not so. The Greek word for "exalted above measure" means "to lift up oneself above." Here it does not mean that Paul was to do so arrogantly in regard to other people, but to do so confidently in regard to the negative circumstances he faced.

Doesn't the verse (in every version) say that the thorn was "the messenger of Satan?" Who did *not* want Paul "exalted?" Satan— that's why he persecuted Paul. Who *did* want Paul lifted up, and who *gave* him the revelation in the first place? God. (By the way, if God knew that the special revelation He gave Paul was going to make him conceited, He never would have given him the revelation in the first place. No loving earthly father would give knowledge to a child if he knew that the child would misuse it and cause himself problems).

II Corinthians 12:8-10 (KJV)

For this thing I besought the Lord thrice, that it might depart from me.

And he said unto me, My grace is sufficient for thee: for my strength is made perfect in weakness. Most gladly therefore will I rather glory in my infirmities, that the power of Christ may rest upon me.

Therefore I take pleasure in infirmities, in reproaches, in necessities, in persecutions, in distresses for Christ's sake: for when I am weak, then am I strong.

Paul recognized that the source of the "thorn" was Satan, and the source of the revelation was the Lord. In verse eight, Paul petitioned the Lord Jesus Christ for the thorn to be removed. Paul said, in effect, "Lord, get these guys off my back!"

The Lord's reply in verse nine is in no way exasperated, snide or any less magnanimous than Jesus always is. The essence of what the Lord said was, "Paul, I cannot totally remove this persecution, but even amidst these circumstances, I will, by my power, accomplish my purposes within you." What Paul later wrote to Timothy confirms this.

II Timothy 3:10, 11

You, however, know all about my teaching, my way of life, my purpose, faith, patience, love, endurance,

Persecutions, sufferings— what kinds of things happened to me in Antioch, Iconium and Lystra, the persecutions I endured. Yet the Lord rescued me from all of them.

A most pertinent verse that must be understood comes to mind at this point:

I Corinthians 10:13

No temptation has seized you except what is common to man. And God is faithful; he will not let you be tempted beyond what you can bear. But when you are tempted, he will also provide a way out so that you can stand up under it.

At this point, we recall Kushner's observation that human experience clearly shows that if God indeed does control the storms of life, He far too often fails to "temper the wind to the shorn lamb" (see Chapter One). Many people believe that I Corinthians 10:13 says that God controls the circumstances in our lives and will not allow them to overwhelm us, but this interpretation contradicts both the Bible and human experience.

The great key to this verse is the word "temptation." It refers to a temptation to *sin*. As Christians, we may go through some very difficult circumstances, but at no time will the temptation to sin be so irresistible that we have no choice but to sin, which makes this a very comforting verse. Please note, however, that the verse does not say that God will always make the temptation go away, but rather that God will provide in such a way that we can endure. The translation by New Testament scholar R.C.H. Lenski is very clear: "...but God is faithful, who will not suffer you to be tempted above your ability, but will make together with the temptation the way out, namely your ability to bear it." [152]

As always, each verse in God's Word must be understood in its context. Throughout I Corinthians Chapter 10, we see that the context regards each believer's choice between the true God and idolatry. As we have seen, it is very difficult for God to help those of His people who do not adhere to His guidance and direction. It would seem that the promise of I Corinthians 10:13— that God will help us not to sin in times of temptation— is available only to those Christians doing their best to keep themselves from idols and obey God.

"No temptation has seized you except what is common to man." Even that alone is comforting. How often does each of us think he's "the Lone Ranger?" A helpful verse that relates to this truth is in I Peter:

I Peter 5:9

Resist him [your enemy the Devil], standing firm in the faith, because you know that your brothers throughout the world are undergoing the same kind of sufferings.

Knowing that Christians everywhere are enduring the same kinds of suffering we are makes it possible for us to help other people who are going through what we have already endured.

As for the rest of I Corinthians 10:13, we see it as illustrative of the truth Paul expressed in II Timothy 3:10,11 that we quoted several paragraphs above. We see it as a promise to help you stay faithful to God's Word, even if you never get out of temptations, and even if you die for your faith as many saints have.

Temptation is not sin, but yielding to it at the expense of God's Word *is* sin. For a Christian who desires to serve the Lord, temptation and persecution "come with the territory." But— God is faithful! He is also able and willing to deliver us. In the midst of any situation, we can be comforted by knowing that our Lord Jesus understands our suffering, and that because He stayed faithful to God's Word, we can do likewise and find the "way out," realizing that because of the spiritual battle we are in, the "way out" might be at the appearing of our Lord.

---

152. R.C.H. Lenski, *The Interpretation of I and II Corinthians* (Augsburg Pub. House, Minneapolis MN, reprint 1963), page 403.

Knowing that he had within him the power of the risen Christ, Paul took a "come-on-give-me-your-best-shot" approach to the trials and tribulations of being a committed Christian.

II Corinthians 12:9b, 10

Therefore I will boast all the more gladly about my weaknesses, so that Christ's power may rest on me.

That is why, for Christ's sake, I delight in weaknesses, in insults, in hardships, in persecutions, in difficulties. For when I am weak, then am I strong.

He is not saying, as the NIV seems to say, that he boasts "about" his sufferings (that would be egotistical), but rather "in" (KJV) the midst of them he boasts in the power of Christ at work within him. Here once again is this vital key to Christian living: meet adversity head on, realize your absolute *"self-helplessness"* and move ahead with the Lord, so that He can energize His power in you.

Keep Your Eyes On The Goal

Not only does God not cause us suffering, He helps us endure it by giving us great hope of deliverance. The principle of hope permeates our everyday lives. Ever gone to a highly-recommended restaurant for the first time? Could you see it from your home? If not, why did you bother to get in your car and head out in search of it? Hope of reward. As you drove, did you worry that the restaurant might not actually exist? Probably not. Why? Because people told you it was there. In other words, your hope was based upon something relatively concrete: someone's word that Big Bubba's Burger Bastion was indeed real.

Suppose they had told you that there were great burgers at "some restaurant somewhere." Could you leave home with that nebulous hope? Yes, but how long do you think you would persevere, and how easily distracted do you think you would be by Pepperoni Pete's Pizza Parlor you would keep passing as you drove in circles? The point is that the more valuable you anticipate the rewards to be and the more real your hope of them is, the more diligently you will pursue the right directions, avoid the wrong directions and keep going until you reach your goal.

Hebrews 12:2-4

Let us fix our eyes on Jesus, the author and perfecter of our faith, who for the joy set before him endured the cross, scorning its shame, and sat down at the right hand of the throne of God.

Consider him who endured such opposition from sinful men, so that you will not grow weary and lose heart.

In your struggle against sin, you have not yet resisted to the point of shedding your blood.

As with every aspect of life, Jesus Christ is our perfect example of living in the light of hope. What was Jesus Christ's hope? What was "the joy set before Him" that enabled Him to endure the cross? It was God's promise to Him, set forth in many Old Testament verses (such as Psalm 2:8,9; 16:10; Daniel 7:13, 14; et al), that if He were faithful unto the death of the cross, God would raise Him from the dead and exalt Him as the King of a "new world order." We too have God's promise that we will live forever in Paradise, enjoying the rewards of our labors in this life. Let us emulate our Lord's example and keep our eyes on the right goal.

The Apostle Paul is perhaps the second most vivid biblical example of a believer focused on the hope God had given him. Consider what he wrote in the following verses:

II Corinthians 4:16,17

Therefore we do not lose heart. Though outwardly we are wasting away, yet inwardly we are being renewed day by day.

For our light and momentary troubles are achieving for us an eternal glory that far outweighs them all.

Would you agree that for Paul, the hope of Christ's appearing and rewarding him was a pretty big deal? If you're not sure, look at his perspective in the following verse:

Romans 8:18

I consider that our present sufferings are not worth comparing with the glory that will be revealed in us.

Were the lashes that bit into Paul's flesh fairly *real* to him? Surely. And yet his absolute assurance of it all being worth it was far more real. It must be available for each Christian to live with that same attitude.

A very important word to note in II Corinthians 4:17 is "momentary." Have you ever heard the statement, "This too will pass"? With regard to any earthly circumstance, it is true. It is imperative that we as Christians resist the world's relentless urging to live life with a short-term-gain perspective: "Drive it now! No payments 'til the turn of the century!" "Drink it now! No payments 'til tomorrow morning!" The irony is that the short-term-gain approach usually cheats us out of both current blessings *and* future rewards. I Timothy 4:8 says that "godliness is profitable now, and in the life that is to come." We must develop a long-term-gain perspective such as Paul had. How can we do so?

II Corinthians 4:18

So we fix our eyes not on what is seen, but on what is unseen. For what is seen is temporary, but what is unseen is eternal.

For the believer, the hope of everlasting life and the rewards that accompany it are inextricably linked.

The theme of rewards for doing what is right and of punishment (for the unbeliever) or loss of potential rewards (for the Christian) runs throughout Scripture. [153] We will all stand before the judgment seat of Christ (Romans 14:10; II Corinthians 5:10). As stated, the word "glory" often relates to the future rewards of the believer (e.g., Romans 8:17; II Timothy 2:10). The hope of everlasting life and the inheritance we will enjoy is to be a major motivation to walk according to God's Word and to keep going until we reach the finish line.

I Peter 1:3-5

Praise be to the God and Father of our Lord Jesus Christ! In his great mercy he has given us new birth into a living hope through the resurrection of Jesus Christ from the dead,

And into an inheritance that can never perish, spoil or fade— kept in heaven for you,

---

153. *Grace Unto Works: The Christian's Reward* (CES Bi-Monthly Tape, Sep/Oct 1992). Also see *The Judgment Seat of Christ*, by Rick Howard (Naioth Sound and Publishing, Woodside CA, 1990).

Who through faith are shielded by God's power until the coming of the salvation that is ready to be revealed in the last time.

Read those fabulous verses again and let them sink into your heart. If those truths don't put a smile on your face, check your pulse. In fact, such wonderful statements could even cause you to *rejoice*.

I Peter 1:6

In this you greatly rejoice, though now for a little while you may have had to suffer grief in all kinds of trials.

Look at the words in that verse, "for a little while." The obstacle you are now facing won't last forever, and perhaps not even until tomorrow. The phrase "you may have had" indicates that often we can stand for God and do His will with no resulting affliction, but that when it does come our way, we can respond to it in light of our hope.

I Peter 1:7 (KJV)

That the trial [test] of your faith, being much more precious than of gold that perisheth, though it be tried with fire, might be found unto praise and honour and glory at the appearing of Jesus Christ:

We are tested in this life, but by His example our Master has instructed us how to deal with every challenge, and He has equipped us with His power to do so. That holy spirit power is also our guarantee that when He appears we will "graduate," and that we can do so with honors. It is the Lord whom we serve and it is He who will reward us (Colossians 3:23-25). Until then, we can live each day with a song of praise in our hearts, no matter how the circumstances surrounding us may fluctuate: "Honey, today I was promoted to President of the company!" Next evening: "Honey, today we had a hostile corporate takeover. I got fired."

Sometimes we may feel as though there's nothing left to go wrong (which in itself is at least a *little* uplifting). We may feel like Habakkuk did when he was asked how his farm was doing. Here is his reply:

Habakkuk 3:17 (KJV)

Although the fig tree shall not blossom, neither shall fruit be in the vines; the labour of the olive shall fail, and the fields shall yield no meat; the flock shall be cut off from the fold, and there shall be no herd in the stalls:

No doubt he then added, "Outside of that, the farm's doing great!"

If it seems that all around us is falling apart, what can we do? What did Habakkuk do?

Habakkuk 3:18, 19a (KJV)

Yet I will rejoice in the Lord, I will joy in the God of my salvation.

The Lord God is my strength, and he will make my feet like hinds' [a deer's] feet, and he will make me to walk upon mine high places.

No matter how bad the circumstances, we can always rejoice in the goodness, grace and love of our heavenly Father and Lord Jesus, for these qualities never change.

James 1:2-4

Consider it pure joy, my brothers, whenever you face trials of many kinds,

Because you know that the testing of your faith develops perseverance.

Perseverance must finish its work so that you may be mature and complete, not lacking anything.

As we stated earlier in the book, the Church Epistles refer to the gift of holy spirit we have received as an "earnest" (II Corinthians 1:22; 5:5; Ephesians 1:14), which means a token, deposit, down-payment or guarantee. You have God's infallible proof that He has supernaturally intervened in your life, and that He and His Son will continue to do so as you walk through this life looking unto them for guidance and help.

Knowing that God is faithful to His Word, that He and Jesus Christ are with us always, and that they are fighting for us in every situation with all they have, we can each diligently do our part in the Body of Christ. We can praise and exalt God and Christ no matter what circumstances surround us. We can pray with confidence in their willingness to help us. We can declare their goodness, their righteousness and their love to all men. Let us do so with great joy and with great enthusiasm.

Let us lay the blame for evil on Satan, where it belongs, and resolve to give him a taste of his impending future defeat by walking boldly with the Lord Jesus Christ. Let us exercise His power within us today, and know that we will live happily ever after with our Father God, our Lord Jesus Christ, and all those who will have believed in them. See you in Paradise!

Topical Index

Bullinger, E. W., 25-26, 35, 52
allegories, 82n
Figures of Speech Used in the Bible, 64
idiomatic usage of permission, 68-73
hardening of Pharoah's heart, 74
Hebrew idioms, 69n
metonymy, classes of, 65n
pistis, translation of, 131-132

C

Calvin, John, 54
Satan
as executor of God's justice, 105
as scapegoat, 54-55n
Carty, Jay, 99
causes versus reasons, 5
change, sorrow as catalyst for, 163-164
character
building, 169-172, 194
of God, 4, 23-24, 35, 41-42, 53
as revealed through Jesus Christ, 59-60
misrepresentation by Satan, 31-34
Old and New Testaments, 55, 58
of Jesus Christ, 26n, 43-44
of Satan, 35, 75, 89, 110-111
before rebellion (Lucifer), 24-27
revealed by Christ, 76
chastening, 163-164
definition of, 161
God's, examples, 162-163
means of, 165

versus punishment, 161
within Christian fellowship, 165
Christ, *see* Jesus Christ
Christians
as God's soldiers, 147-149
as representatives of Christ, 152-153
as soldiers, 185-186, 193
as targets, 189
authority over Satan, 76-77
casting out evil spirits, 57-58
community faith, 151-153
example by response to suffering, 185-188
goals of, 201-202
identification with Jesus Christ, 106
inheritance in age to come, 203-204
obedience to God, 6, 143
persecution of, 55n
perspective toward life, 203
spiritual equipment of, 186-187
Church Age, 97, 107
civil authorities
judgment by, 98
responsibility of, 109-110
classes, Metonymy, n, 65
comfort, 191-192
community faith, 151-153
companionship, 193
confidence, *see* faith
consequences of sin, 102-103, 108-109
contractual agreements with God, 101-102
Conybeare, W. J., 149n
corporal punishment, 160n

I

J

judgments
  by Jesus Christ (future), 97, 107
  God's, 48, 95-96
    based upon faith, 98-99
    on Christians, 96
    present age, 98-99
  man's, 98
justice of God, death of Pharoah's
  firstborn, 105-106

K

Kenyon, E. W., 28, 36, 44
Kushner, Rabbi Harold, 10, 13-19,
  74, 199
  God as comforter, 92-93
  Job's calamities, 86-89
  Job's friends, 83-84

L

Lamb of God, 45
laws
  Biblical versus humanistic,
    109-110
  God's, breaking, 66
Lazarus, raising from dead, 150
leaders, identification with, 106
leadership, praying for, 151
Lenski, R. C. H., 199
The Life and Epistles of St. Paul, 149
literalism versus figurativism, Old
  Testament, 58-60, 61
long-term perspectives versus
  short-term, 203
Lord's Prayer, 146
love, God as, 44

Lucifer, 148
  definition of name, 24n
  freedom of will, 24-27
  other names, 27
  see also Satan, Devil

M

man born blind (John 9: 1-2),
  21-23, 113
manna, purpose of, 156n
Mary, 100
mercy, 100
  of God, 102-103
Meshach, 190
Metonymy, 64-65, 138
  classes of, 65n
  of the Subject, 93, 103-105, 113
    death of Saul, 66-67
    God versus Satan, 67, 75-78
    Old Testament, 76-78
  Prophetic
    hardening of Pharoah's heart,
      73-75
    versus idiomatic usage of
      permission, 69-72
miracles
  Christian unity/faith relationship,
    142-143
  God's timing of, 141
  relationship with faith, 139-143
  water from the rock, 140
miserable comforters, Job's, 83-87,
  137
moral behavior, 13
Morris, John, 17
Moses, 100, 140

Christian example in response to, 187-188

comfort in times of, 191-192

companionship in, 192

correlation with glory, 189

definition of, 183-184

deliverance from, 91

due to bad leadership, 151

end of, 47-50

for doing good, 188-189

holding God responsible for, 1-3

hope of deliverance, 201-202

innocent victims of, 86, 92

accusing, 83- 85

material wealth, 184

of child as result of parental sin, 112-114

of Jesus Christ, 180, 192-193

rationalization of, 16

rejoicing in, 204-205

Satan as source of, 29, 54-55n

theories of

as Divine Plan, 12-13

as educational tool, 14-15

as privilege, 12

as test, 15-16, 41-42, 184, 189

God as cause of, 10-13, 16-17, 82, 155, 161

undeserved, rewards, 12n

T-U

tares, parable of, 97

temptation

of Jesus Christ, 111, 172-173

overcoming, 199-200

versus sin, 200

tempting God, 156

testing God's Word, 171-174

tests

God's

New Testament, 170-171

Old Testament, 168-170

versus Satan's, 167-168

of faith, 173-174

suffering as, 15-16, 184, 189

"theistic" evolution, 18

theory of evolution, 17-19

thorn in the flesh (Paul), 197-199

timing of answers to prayers, 148-151

tragedy, *see* suffering

translations, Biblical, 22-23

trust, 156

losing, Israel in the wilderness, 155-156

of Jesus Christ in His Father, 158-160

see also faith

truth of God's Word, 51-53, 58-61

V

variable sin, 99

Vine's Expository Dictionary of New Testament Words, 131

visions, 197n

W

warfare, spiritual

Christian authority over Satan, 76-77

Christians as targets, 189

importance of prayer, 147-149

What Is Christian Educational Services?

Christian Educational Services, (CES) is a non-profit, tax exempt United States (Indiana) corporation whose purposes are to make known the Word of God, to further the gospel of the Lord Jesus Christ, to facilitate fellowship among Christians and to provide Christian educational services, including biblical research, written publications and biblical teachings. We do this via live speakers, tapes and literature. Our teachings point people to the Lordship of Jesus Christ in their lives. We encourage Christians to apply these teachings in their local areas in community with other likeminded believers.

The basis for all our efforts is the Bible, which we believe to be the Word of God, perfect in its original writing. So-called errors, contradictions or discrepancies are the result of man's subsequent interference in the transmission of the text, mistranslations or failure to understand what is written. CES draws from all relevant sources that shed light on the integrity of Scripture, whether in the field of geography, customs, language, history, or principles governing Bible interpretation. Our goal is to seek the truth without respect to tradition or "orthodoxy."

Any individual willing to examine his beliefs in the light of God's Word will perhaps profit from our teachings. They are non-denominational, and are intended to strengthen one's faith in God, Jesus Christ, and the Bible, no matter what his denominational preference may be. Designed primarily for individual home study, the teachings are the result of intensive research and rational methods, making them easy to follow, verify and practically apply. When accurately understood, the Word of God brings great deliverance from fear, doubt and worry, and leads the individual Christian to genuine freedom, confidence and joy in living. Beyond such practical blessings, however, our goal is to enable the student to do biblical research for himself, so he is able to develop his own convictions, separate truth from error, and become an effective communicator of God's Word.

Biblical materials produced by CES are designed to assist individual spiritual growth as well as support local fellowships and churches in the CES Fellowship Community. Our goal is to provide healthy biblical teaching, and to help people enjoy the fruits of salvation and authentic Christ-like living.

To receive our free bimonthly newsletter, *The Sower,* or a complete listing of our materials, please contact us at:

Christian Educational Services
2144 East 52nd Street
Indianapolis, Indiana 46205
888-255-6189
CES@CESonline.org
www.CESonline.org

We look forward to hearing from you!

Books

The Christian's Hope: The Anchor of the Soul – What the Bible really says about Death, Judgment, Rewards, Heaven, and the Future Life on a Restored Earth

The Gift of Holy Spirit: Every Christian's Divine Deposit

Is There Death After Life?

One God & One Lord: Reconsidering the Cornerstone of the Christian Faith

Sex & Scripture: A Biblical Study of Proper Sexual Behavior

Publications

22 Principles of Bible Interpretation or How to Eliminate Apparent Bible Contradictions

Beyond a Reasonable Doubt: 23 Arguments for the Historical Validity of the Resurrection of Jesus Christ

Becoming a Christian: Why? What? How?

Righteousness—Every Christian's Gift from God

What is True Baptism?

23 Reasons to Believe in a Rapture before the Great Tribulation or Why We Aren't in the Tribulation Now

24 Reasons Why Salvation is Permanent for Christians

34 Reasons Why the Holy Spirit is Not a Separate "Person" From the Only True God, The Father

46 Reasons Why our Heavenly Father has no Equals or "Co-Equals"

Defending Dispensationalism: Standing Fast in the Liberty

The Death Penalty: Godly or Ungodly?

The Bible - You Can Believe It

Audio Tape Seminars

New Life in Christ—Foundations for Powerful Christian Living (15 hrs)

The Creation-Evolution Controversy (6 hrs)

Growing Up in Christ, Part One: The Fruit of the Spirit— Developing the Character of Christ (12 hrs)

Growing Up in Christ, Part Two: Teaching and Activation in the Manifestations of the Gift of Holy Spirit (9 hrs)

Introduction to God's Heart (24 hrs)

A Journey through the Old Testament (26 hrs)

Romans (18 hrs)

The Book of Revelation (9 hrs)

Jesus Christ, the Diameter of the Ages (6 hrs)

Truth or Tradition? (12 hrs)

**Be sure to visit us online at:
www.TruthOrTradition.com**